"Dr. Brenda Salter McNeil is a legend. She's one of the church's greatest thinkers on one of the world's greatest challenges—reconciliation. Fifty years ago Dr. King lamented that the most segregated hour in the world is eleven o'clock on Sunday morning. Here is Dr. Salter McNeil's plan to change that. There could be no better time for this book to release than now as we see a new movement for racial justice sweeping across this country. Read this book and get ready for a holy revolution."

Shane Claiborne, author, speaker, activist

"*Roadmap to Reconciliation* is both practical and deeply theological, and a welcome addition to the ministry of reconciliation. Drawing from qualitative data as well as practical experience, Dr. Brenda Salter McNeil offers a step-by-step process for reconciliation that both new and seasoned reconcilers will find profoundly useful. For the newcomer, Salter McNeil shines a light on the often enigmatic and challenging path toward reconciliation, uncovering potential pitfalls. For the road-weary old-timer, she dips into the well of her experiences as a lifelong reconciler to offer wisdom that promises to demystify the process and bring hope to even the most cynical. I recommend this book as a practical handbook for small groups, leaders and anyone willing to engage in justice-based reconciliation."

Christena Cleveland, Center for Reconciliation, Duke Divinity School, author of *Disunity in Christ*

"For Dr. Brenda Salter McNeil, reconciliation is not a catchphrase—it's a byword! That's because Brenda has always understood reconciliation as a journey and not an event, which is something still very popular in Christian thinking today. In this book Brenda has not only captured some of the scenery along the way, but has set the backdrop for the trip in a biblical frame as only she can. It's an excursion into life abundant, a pilgrimage that Brenda has been on for many years, in many contexts, with scores of people from many ethnicities and experiences. It needs to be our journey too."

Terry LeBlanc, executive director, Indigenous Pathways

"We've heard it said, 'The road to hell is paved with good intentions.' Sadly, 'good intentions' are all many of our churches can boast of when it comes to the ministry of reconciliation imparted to us by Christ. This book is a rare gift in holding forth not just a compelling vision for communities of reconciliation, but a practical course of action to achieve it. Following the *Roadmap to Reconciliation*, so powerfully and honestly laid out by Brenda Salter McNeil, has the potential to help restore the integrity of our churches as outposts of God's kingdom. All we need now are leaders and churches willing to embark on a journey beyond good intentions!"

JR Rozko, Missio Alliance

"*Roadmap to Reconciliation* is a labor of love, commitment and calling.... The time is right for our world to receive the fruit of Dr. Brenda's many years of work, study and experience in being a champion for racial reconciliation. We are desperate, not only for a biblical and theological rationale for unity, wholeness and justice, but also for a substantive and practical way forward. This book has it all!"

Ruth Haley Barton, founder, Transforming Center, author of *Life Together in Christ*

"Dr. Brenda Salter McNeil is one of the most credible and prophetic voices of our time. In *Roadmap to Reconciliation*—the fruit and culmination of more than twenty-five years of personal, practical and pioneering effort—she explains why we must and how we can get beyond rhetoric to results in pursuit of individual and corporate transformation beyond the distinctions of this world that so often and otherwise divide. Grounded in biblical and experiential knowledge, *Roadmap to Reconciliation* will help you recognize that lament, confession, reconciliation and justice are not peripheral to the gospel but intrinsic to it, and more than that, it offers the ways and means to advance hope in an increasingly diverse and cynical society."

Mark DeYmaz, Mosaic Church, author of *Building a Healthy Multi-ethnic Church*

"*Roadmap to Reconciliation* is a gift to Christ's church on many levels. It has biblical, sociological and theological depth. It is written with the passion of someone who has given her life to understanding and engaging the profound messiness of racial reconciliation and justice, someone who lives exactly as she preaches. If you are a leader of a Christian ministry or church, if you are an individual or small group who is ready take the plunge into the mission of reconciliation and justice, if you are already on the journey and need to discover where you are and how to take the next steps, you will be challenged, blessed and empowered as you read, and most importantly, as you apply what you read. God will give you encouragement and direction each step of the way."

Jim Lundgren, former interim president, InterVarsity Christian Fellowship

"If anyone knows the roadmap to reconciliation, it's Dr. Brenda Salter McNeil. She has personally walked this road, preached on this road, healed on this road and built multicultural relationships of love and partnership on this road. I am privileged to have intersected in ministry with Dr. Brenda while walking together on this same road toward reconciliation. You will gain much wisdom from the *Roadmap to Reconciliation* with Dr. Brenda as a very capable guide."

David Anderson, founder and senior pastor, Bridgeway Community Church, author of *Gracism*

"A roadmap to reconciliation is needed for every community, whether domestic or global, whether working with students in elite universities or urban churches on the west side of Chicago. Rev. Dr. Brenda's decades of mobilizing reconcilers and consulting with organizations give us helpful pictures and insight into practical steps for transformation. Her insightful diagram of landmarks in the journey of reconciliation is worth the entire book!"

Sandra Maria Van Opstal, associate pastor, Grace and Peace Community, author of *The Next Worship*

"The journey of reconciliation often takes us to valleys and wilderness, places of despair and disorientation. In this invaluable book, Dr. Brenda Salter McNeil offers us a roadmap that is full of biblical wisdom and practical insights. The map does not promise to make the journey easier or safer. Prophetically, it shows us the way forward, exhorting us to continue this costly journey of discipleship."

Peter Cha, associate professor of pastoral theology, Trinity Evangelical Divinity School

"*Roadmap to Reconciliation* is a tremendous resource, filled with practical tips born out of decades of life in the trenches. Dr. Brenda's integrity, wisdom, character and life shine through these pages. Thank you, Brenda, for such a wonderful gift!"

Pete Scazzero, author of *Emotionally Healthy Spirituality* and *The Emotionally Healthy Leader*

"With clarity, precision and resolution, the Rev. Dr. Brenda Salter McNeil has provided for the faithful traveler a most-needed compass and map toward what God in Christ has given to the church—the service of reconciliation. Theological in analysis and practical in application, this text exposes and expands Brenda's heartbeat and mission as a prophetic and pastoral voice of unity, integrity and justice. . . . A must-have for every Christian pedestrian."

Luis A. Carlo, professor of urban studies and religion and education, Alliance Theological Seminary, NYC

"I've had the privilege of working with Dr. Brenda Salter McNeil as she delivers biblical insight and practical application to the process of developing racial and ethnic reconciliation. Her years of experience have paved a way for many campus, church and civic leaders who desire a better way forward. Her passion for reconciliation is rooted in Scripture and her life's work is a testament of God's ability to change hearts and transform communities."

Walter "Woody" Webb, VP for Student Development, Olivet Nazarene University

"Dr. Brenda is arguably one of the leading voices on reconciliation in our country today. She is honest, humble, credible and the right leader to influence many on this timely and important topic in today's culture. Listen to her and learn from her!"

Brad Lomenick, author of *The Catalyst Leader* and *H3 Leadership*

"Comprehensive, personal and systematic, *Roadmap to Reconciliation* truly is a compendium of Dr. Brenda's life work! Dr. Brenda invites us to join her on the very road on which she embarked many years ago. Like a wise guide she gives us a vision of where we are going, describes the significant landmarks, warns of the difficult places along the way and remains ever hopeful that we will reach our destiny together. Sprinkled with theory and framework, stories and reflections, *Roadmap to Reconciliation* is the perfect resource for academics theorizing about reconciliation, professors seeking tools for reconciliation studies and practitioners committed to building and sustaining reconciling communities."

Jeanne Porter King, global leadership consultant and president, TransPorter Group, Inc.

"Everything I know about Dr. Brenda Salter McNeil reflects her godly spirit of compassion, mercy and justice. In fact, she's a major reason why I continue to believe that the gospel ministry of reconciliation can bring transformation in our increasingly divided world. Brenda is one of the most important leaders we have today on issues of racial righteousness and diversity in the church, and I have no doubt that this book will help others on their journeys toward a deeper and more complete faith."

Edward Gilbreath, author of *Reconciliation Blues*

"The church needs to recover the systemic realities of justice, advocacy and power that biblical reconciliation was always meant to address if we are going to embody true reconciliation and racial justice. If your ministry knows that you should and could do more to live out your commitment to reconciliation and racial justice but is not sure how to take the next step, this book will guide you on that journey. *Roadmap to Reconciliation 2.0* will help you plan for and implement a systemic shift toward faithfulness around reconciliation, race and faith that will bless your ministry and build God's kingdom!"

Liz Mosbo VerHage, associate pastor of global and local ministries, Quest Church, Seattle

"If you liked Dr. Brenda Salter McNeil's book *Roadmap to Reconciliation,* you are going to love *Roadmap to Reconciliation 2.0*! It dives deeper and gives more content into how we pursue this path to reconciliation, while nuancing how the journey is different for people of color and allies who are trying to walk alongside us. This book takes seriously the need for self-care, restoration and being recharged and refilled by the Spirit to be healthy and have longevity in the ministry of reconciliation. If your church or ministry organization is ready to go deeper in your reconciliation journey, this book is for you!"

Dominique Gilliard, Evangelical Covenant Church director of racial righteousness and reconciliation, author of *Rethinking Incarceration*

"The journey toward engaging deeper levels of reconciliation is important, but one also fraught with unforeseen land mines. Organizations looking to walk this path are wise to learn from those who have gone before them and to rely on curriculum that will help steer them through these complicated waters. *Roadmap to Reconciliation 2.0* is the fruit of over three decades of lived experience. If your group is looking to undertake a journey to more deeply and authentically engage with reconciliation, you should read this book!"

Daniel Hill, senior pastor of River City Community Church, Chicago, author of *White Awake*

"Our church has pursued racial reconciliation and racial justice for several years, and *Roadmap to Reconciliation* has helped us honestly evaluate ourselves, our leadership structure, church culture, discipleship practices, and outreach activities in our neighborhood and city. This book will push your church to repent and reflect on individual and systemic injustices. In short, *Roadmap to Reconciliation 2.0* is a model for becoming a long-term reconciling community. I highly recommend it!"

Won Kim, director of discipleship, New Community Church, Chicago

"This book continues to solidify Dr. Brenda Salter McNeil as a practical theologian and a prophetic voice of biblical reconciliation and justice. Her insights and wisdom within this resource are a powerful classroom of unifying principles and concepts. Everything she writes should be read and applied by people of faith that we might be a force of transformation in a broken and divided world."

Efrem Smith, president and CEO, World Impact, author of *The Post-Black and Post-White Church*

"I find in . . . Brenda Salter McNeil a rugged commitment to the church and to the centrality of the gospel and the church in the process of reconciliation. . . . Brenda's book is short and nothing less than a handbook—brief, accessible, illustrated, clear. A handbook that articulates stages in the process of reconciliation, and hence it is as useful for those seeking to embody reconciliation in a local church as it is for those who want to be more publicly active."

Scot McKnight, *Patheos,* December 17, 2015

"Deep wrongs need to be made right. All the more, the wrongs we've committed against others need to be healed to the degree that we not only respect one another but earnestly desire and labor for one another to flourish to the fullest of all God intends for his creation. That is what Dr. Brenda is teaching me, and that is what she teaches in *Roadmap to Reconciliation.* Dr. Brenda gives us her life's work in these pages, and it will be my mission to ensure that her instruction is spread far and wide, even to the most hardhearted and privileged among us. Reconciliation is love as Jesus loves. It's a foretaste of the kingdom, now and to come."

Bethany H. Hoang, adviser, IJM and Q Ideas, author of *Deepening the Soul for Justice*

"The world's most authentic and inspiring reconciler shows believers how to stop talking about reconciliation—and start *being* it together. Gripping to read and exciting to receive, Dr. Brenda Salter McNeil's roadmap on how to reconcile offers a wake-up call and a course map on how to apply biblical principles to coalesce our racially divided and unjust world by building peacemaking communities rightly engaged for Christ. Passionate, equipping and downright brilliant."

Patricia Raybon, author of *My First White Friend* and *Undivided*

"More than ever, our polarized world needs Dr. Brenda's voice. Her love and respect for people creates a healing place to express our hopes, fears, dreams and confusion. We all want reconciliation—our hearts long for it—but most of us do not know where to start. Brenda patiently and humbly guides our journey toward peace."

Roy Goble, CEO, Goble Properties, cofounder and CEO, PathLight International

"I consider Dr. Brenda Salter McNeil to be one of the great national communicators in the American church. She is the most qualified person I know to write about the topic of race and reconciliation. Her book is extraordinarily timely."

Mac Pier, CEO and founder, The NYC Leadership Center, Lausanne Senior Associate for Cities

"Dr. Brenda Salter McNeil is one of the most admired and powerful witnesses to the ministry of reconciliation in the United States. *Roadmap to Reconciliation* is Brenda Salter McNeil's magnum opus! Here she distills for us the wisdom of a life's work of significant reconciliation engagement with congregations, universities, denominations and communities. Salter McNeil calls us to embrace transformed worldviews and practical action. Pastors, seminarians, lay leaders, university students, activists and anyone hoping for a more reconciled world should read this book!"

Curtiss Paul DeYoung, executive director of Community Renewal Society, Chicago

"For more than two decades I have listened to the voice of Dr. Brenda Salter McNeil. Because she is honest, I have heard things spoken in a timbre of truth. Because she is a prophet, I have heard things I don't always want to hear. Because she is one of the great living preachers of the day, I have heard things articulated with gospel clarity. Because she is a trusted friend, I have heard things spoken in fierce love. Because she is a teacher of reconciliation, I have seen her stand in contested places with bold, unwavering courage. Her voice is to be trusted, heard and honored. Read her words and listen for a voice of wise and honest truth. Listen. She writes words we need to hear."

Keith Anderson, president, The Seattle School of Theology & Psychology, author of *Spirituality of Listening*

"Racism runs the length of human history and emerges out of the brokenness of every human heart. *Roadmap to Reconciliation* conveys the weight and wisdom of seasoned experience in the face of this painful reality. As compelling theologically and relationally as God's reconciling way may be, Dr. Brenda Salter McNeil helps us see that the pursuit of personal and systemic reconciliation requires more than ordinary Christian discipleship can bear or imagine. She underscores the gifts that can make all the difference: God's reconciling love in Christ, the humble repentance and re-creation of God's people as daily reconcilers, and the long, steady faithfulness of God's reconciling power through sustained practices by those who seek a world of reconciliation, mercy and justice. We are offered here a road to reconciliation marked by profound, sober and credible hope. This is the only kind of map that could be trusted."

Mark Labberton, president, Fuller Theological Seminary

"While many evangelicals express angst over a perceived decline of Christianity in the United States, there is a burgeoning movement of reconciliation that is capturing the imagination of a new generation of believers. The ministry of reconciliation sorely needs an ecclesial center and Dr. Brenda Salter McNeil presents this text as a positive response. This book offers helpful categories to sharpen our discussions and useful exercises that are both practical and applicable. Dr. Salter McNeil provides a roadmap to reconciliation that needs to be embraced by Christians who seek a way forward."

Soong-Chan Rah, North Park Theological Seminary, author of *The Next Evangelicalism* and *Prophetic Lament*

"As a member of our board, Dr. Brenda Salter McNeil has challenged Wycliffe Bible Translators USA to better understand our work of Bible translation in the context of the global narrative of church community, and her new book will do the same for readers. Her heart for justice and reconciliation shines through this book, and she will inspire you as she has inspired us."

Bob Creson, president and CEO, Wycliffe USA

"In our desire to be agents of reconciliation in our neighborhoods as well as our churches, where do we begin? . . . In *Roadmap to Reconciliation* Dr. Brenda provides not only a compelling call for biblical reconciliation, but practical ways we can grow in our understanding of racial injustice and social inequity and begin to engage in these complex issues. . . . Reading this book is like taking a journey with an experienced reconciliation docent who knows the path and leads the way, pointing out what is significant and life-changing along the way. This book is a must-read for those of us in the church who want to pursue justice."

Nancy Sugikawa, associate pastor, Lighthouse Christian Church, Bellevue, Washington

ROADMAP TO RECONCILIATION

MOVING COMMUNITIES INTO UNITY, WHOLENESS AND JUSTICE

Foreword by EUGENE CHO

BRENDA SALTER McNEIL

With contributions by J. DEREK McNEIL

An imprint of InterVarsity Press
Downers Grove, Illinois

InterVarsity Press
P.O. Box 1400, Downers Grove, IL 60515-1426
ivpress.com
email@ivpress.com

Second edition ©2020 by Brenda Salter McNeil
First edition ©2015 by Brenda Salter McNeil

InterVarsity Press® is the book-publishing division of InterVarsity Christian Fellowship/USA®, a movement of students and faculty active on campus at hundreds of universities, colleges, and schools of nursing in the United States of America, and a member movement of the International Fellowship of Evangelical Students. For information about local and regional activities, visit intervarsity.org.

Scripture quotations, unless otherwise noted, are from the New Revised Standard Version of the Bible, copyright 1989 by the Division of Christian Education of the National Council of the Churches of Christ in the USA. Used by permission. All rights reserved.

While any stories in this book are true, some names and identifying information may have been changed to protect the privacy of individuals.

Author photo by Zac Davis. Makeup by ILCK Artistry.

Cover design and image composite: David Fassett
Interior design: Beth McGill
Images: mountain range with star sky: © Phaitoon Sutunyawatchai / Moment Collection / Getty Images
   hypnotic background: © Michel Tripepi / EyeEm / Getty Images
   winding road: © Paul Carroll and Mhairi Carroll / Moment Collection / Getty Images
   postage stamp border: © troyek / E+ / Getty Images
   clouds: © Nattawut Lakjit / EyeEm /Getty Images

ISBN 978-0-8308-4812-6 (print)
ISBN 978-0-8308-4813-3 (digital)

Printed in the United States of America ∞

Library of Congress Cataloging-in-Publication Data
A catalog record for this book is available from the Library of Congress.

P	20	19	18	17	16	15	14	13	12	11	10	9	8	7	6	5	4	3	2
Y	37	36	35	34	33	32	31	30	29	28	27	26	25	24	23	22	21	20	

I dedicate this book to the memory of my mother,

Dorothy Elizabeth Mitchell Salter,
with love and gratitude for her parenting,
prayers and perseverance,

and to Catherine Meyer Headington,
who invested in me and saw the potential
of who I could become.

I am who I am today because of them.

*We are caught in an inescapable network of mutuality,
tied in a single garment of destiny. Whatever affects
one directly, affects all indirectly.*

Rev. Dr. Martin Luther King Jr.

Letter from a Birmingham Jail

CONTENTS

FOREWORD

Eugene Cho

*R*econciliation. Let's be honest. Reconciliation has become a trendy topic of conversation . . . which isn't necessarily a bad thing. People are talking about it and that's good. There are gatherings, teachings, sermons, classes and entire conferences around the subject of reconciliation. But, if we're not careful, it is quite possible and tempting to be more in love with the idea of reconciliation than to actually engage in the actual work of reconciliation—the arduous, painful and messy marathon work of reconciliation. That's the pivotal question we must ask: Are we more in love with the idea of following Jesus than actually following Jesus—including to and through some difficult areas?

One of my favorite (which often means challenging) stories from the Scriptures comes from John 4. One can talk about Samaria, theologize about Samaria, preach about Samaria, liturgize about Samaria, sing about Samaria . . . but one can still do all those things and still not walk through Samaria.

And this is precisely why *Roadmap to Reconciliation* by Dr. Brenda Salter McNeil is such an important book and resource. Salter McNeil not only does the critical job of explaining the vision of reconciliation but, equally as important, guides us through the practical steps of actually moving forward and toward reconciliation while constantly reminding us of the vision.

And while I certainly appreciate and applaud the practicalities of this book, I'm especially grateful for the honesty and realness because the last thing we need is a glamorized or romanticized vision of reconciliation. Anyone who conveys that reconciliation work is easy either isn't on that journey or is trying to sell something.

But the book's foremost credibility is directly associated with the integrity of the person who's inviting us to this journey of reconciliation. I prefer not to use words like *leading, expert, guru* or whatever other elevated phrases we use to describe people. What I know—as a longtime friend, fellow pastor and colleague in kingdom ministry—is that Salter McNeil walks the walk. For her, this isn't just a course she teaches as a university professor, a sermon she preaches at a church or a set of consulting principles she imparts to institutions or organizations. This is a calling, a deep conviction and a journey she has devoted much of her life to, and it has permeated every aspect of her life.

We can all agree we are living in challenging times that demand the important and critical work of reconciliation. While it's possible we may have a trajectory of where we need to go, we don't quite know *how* to get there. We need a map. We need a guide. We need a roadmap to reconciliation.

PREFACE TO THE REVISED EDITION

At some point, I begin to doubt myself. My own sense of confidence begins to wane, and I begin to wonder whether I actually was any good in the first place!" These were the words of a dear friend and ministry colleague describing what happens to people who find themselves drafted to lead the reconciliation initiative in their church, organization or academic institution.

I responded by saying that, in my experience, these people are often expected to be experts, but they have not been adequately trained or equipped to lead systemic change regarding diversity, equity and inclusion. They are generally people of color and folks who have a heart for reconciliation, but they struggle to know how to lead a change process.

My friend agreed and said that oftentimes when these people leave they feel like "washed-up NBA players." She explained the analogy like this: "I'm in the NBA, but I get put on a team that does not know how to use my skills. I find myself sitting on the bench most of the time, and then I get traded because I'm not showing that I was worth whatever they paid to draft me. Then I go to another team, and another, and another."

When she said that to me, I almost wept because I know far too many people who fit this description. It's not fair what is happening to the people who are asked to lead the reconciliation effort without having any real guidance or training. And if, in NBA terms, they get "traded," they're often told they're not a good fit or that they weren't collaborative enough—and everyone begins to wonder whether reconciliation is possible at all.

That's why I've updated *Roadmap to Reconciliation*! I'm committed to empowering other people to stay on the reconciliation journey. I know firsthand that there is an emotional, physical and spiritual toll placed on those of us who embody this work. After watching many people struggle to lead this effort, I've come to believe that we need a new way forward that takes this reality more seriously. Therefore, I'm proposing a new paradigm for us in this book that involves the following three core principles:

1. Reconciliation happens by repairing broken systems.

2. Reconciliation happens by engaging power.

3. Reconciliation is not just focusing on relationships and feelings.

Since I believe that reconciliation is an ongoing spiritual process, I'm still on the journey too! This continued commitment to my own growth and transformation has led me to update two parts of the reconciliation process laid out in this book. The first change is the addition of the restoration phase to my roadmap graphic. The book is updated throughout to reflect that new phase. I've also added a new chapter (eight) to talk about how restoration fits into the process. This goes back to what I said earlier—that people who champion reconciliation need opportunities to be restored.

The second update is to explain more deeply what is entailed in the activation phase. Originally I wrote that this phase was "actively working for reconciliation," but I later realized that activation is better understood as "repairing broken systems together," the theme of chapter eight.

Looking over my thirty years of experience now, I know one thing for sure: people need access to resources that strengthen and enhance their ability to be successful and have longevity in reconciliation. This is my life's work; I've been called to inspire and empower the next generation of Christian leaders to be practitioners of reconciliation in their spheres of influence. I'm confident this book will help you do that!

Introduction

A PROPHETIC JOURNEY

*The task of prophetic ministry is to nurture, nourish and evoke
a consciousness and perception alternative to the consciousness
and perception of the dominant culture around us. . . .*

*The alternative consciousness to be nurtured, on the one hand,
serves to criticize in dismantling the dominant consciousness. . . .
On the other hand, that alternative consciousness to be nurtured
serves to energize persons and communities by its promise of
another time and situation toward which the community of
faith may move.*

Walter Brueggemann

||||➤

Where have you been? Why haven't you helped us?" Mavis
shouted at us.

Over twenty years ago my husband and I found ourselves in the
British city of Birmingham, the second most populous urban area
in the United Kingdom and home to a large number of Jamaican
residents.

We had been traveling in England for three weeks with a group of African American seminarians and church leaders. It was exhausting and exhilarating in equal measure. We lectured on issues pertaining to the black church in classrooms, preached in churches, dialogued with police, gave radio interviews, talked with civic and community leaders—all in partnership with the Oxford Centre for Mission Studies.

I had really been looking forward to this particular part of our trip. I thought this meeting in the Jamaican community would be the place where we would receive our warmest welcome. We were going to be with other black people! It would be a chance to rest, rejuvenate and let down our guard. I had imagined that we would be laughing and relaxing together in no time over good food and good music.

We pulled up at the church building in our rundown van, and a large group of Jamaican young people were waiting for us outside. But after we filed into the church and sat through some brief introductions, a young woman stood up and literally began shouting at us.

Why didn't you come sooner?

Didn't you know *what we were going through?*

We sat in complete silence, dumbfounded. We honestly had had no idea of their struggle and no sense of their expectations coming into this gathering. So we just listened as this passionate Christian woman educated us on the history and the plight of the black British people.

We learned from Mavis that after World War II, the British government had encouraged mass immigration from the countries of the British Empire and Commonwealth to fill the shortages in England's labor market. Many Jamaicans and West Indians came with the hope of making a better life for themselves and a brighter future for their children. However, instead of being embraced and received as equal members of society, as was promised by the 1948 British Nationality Act, the Jamaicans and other immigrants found that they were relegated to a low status in the economic and racial class system of England, with no hope of ever being fully accepted as "British."

Even as their children grew, married and started families of their own, they were essentially foreigners in their own land. And to add insult to injury, being born and raised in England meant that they were considered foreigners in Jamaica as well. Can you *imagine* the frustration that would fester from this lack of identity? Coupled with the injustice of economic deprivation and racial discrimination, this frustration led to violence when young Jamaicans took to the streets to protest in 1981. The status quo unfortunately persisted, however, and a second riot had erupted in 1985, just a year before our visit.

We showed up at their church in 1986, and here was Mavis demanding to know what had taken us so long! Why hadn't we come sooner to lend our voices and raise awareness about the conditions they were facing? Were we indifferent to their suffering? Our silence was deafening to them.

Honestly, it was awkward in the church that day, and none of us had any answers for Mavis. We had been *absolutely* clueless. We were aware of the social realities in the United States. We were aware of the racial tensions and inequality in our own country, but we hadn't realized that there were people in other countries around the world who *needed* us. We were uninformed about the racial, social and political plight of our black brothers and sisters in Britain. And to tell you the embarrassing truth, I hadn't taken any interest before that day.

Their news had yet to break through into our circles in the United States. We didn't see ourselves as global citizens, nor did we strongly identify with others of the African Diaspora. We were just *beginning* to reap the benefits of the sacrifices made by the generations before us in the United States. We were just *starting* to enjoy some economic stability, increased access to educational opportunities and greater political and social influence. We hadn't even considered looking outward. Our knowledge of the rest of the world was woefully underdeveloped.

Mavis's questions disturbed us. They indicted us. But they also allowed us to see ourselves through her eyes. These young "black Brits" were in the midst of their own civil rights movement, and they felt abandoned by us. They felt abandoned by the black American church.

We learned such a valuable lesson that day. We learned that *our* story was part of *their* story. We learned that we were part of a larger global narrative and that people needed us. I think we all returned home with a new understanding of ourselves as global citizens. At least *I* did. I came home with the knowledge that I could no longer think of reconciliation in merely nationalistic terms. The world was changing, and I needed some new tools so that I could support folks like Mavis and her friends.

JOURNEYING TOGETHER

England was my wake-up call. That was when I realized that the world is demanding something more of me. That was also when I realized that the world is demanding something more of the church. People like Mavis are watching us and wondering why we remain silent on the critical social issues of our day. Why aren't we more involved? Why aren't we pitching in to solve the problems of racial injustice, gender disparity and social inequity in our world? When unarmed young black men are shot and killed in the United States, why are so many Christians silent as we watch these events unfold? When over 200 schoolgirls are abducted in Nigeria or 148 college students are shot to death in Kenya or 43 abducted in Mexico, why is the Christian community not standing in greater solidarity with them? Mavis would have every right, still today, to look us in the eye and demand answers.

Where have you been, and why have you been so indifferent to the suffering of God's people?

It's time for the followers of Jesus to embark on the prophetic journey that leads to reconciliation and transformation around the world. Many of us may already be aware of the need for reconciliation in our own backyard. We understand the realities playing out in our own neighborhood, our schools, workplace, political system and culture at large. But a lot of us don't recognize the prophetic role we can play both at home and abroad. We aren't yet fully aware of injustices and inequality in our communities, and this understanding and awareness is *absolutely* essential if we are to be God's agents of reconciliation. We cannot ignore the plight of the people around us, and as globalization continues its relentless march onward, we cannot turn a blind eye to the world beyond our national borders either. We have to face the realities here at home, and we must also embrace the stories of people all around the world.

There is a growing group of young Christian leaders who long to heed this prophetic call to local and global reconciliation. And many of us have tried desperately over the years to build communities of reconciliation on our own, relying on trial and error and a mix of reconciliation models like "embracing cultural diversity" and "tolerance-based education." But these models haven't been sustainable in the long run and have left Christian leaders feeling depleted and doubting that we can actually lead people to the kingdom vision of racial, ethnic and gender reconciliation.

We need a clear sense of direction. Where are we going and how will we get there? We can see the inequality and the injustice in our lives and in the world, and we are ready to rise up. But how? How exactly do we *do* this? How exactly does one reconcile? What is the process? What are the practical steps? We see the need, and we believe we have been called to reconciliation, but we don't know how to go about it. We lack the tools, models and practical examples that can show us the way forward. We don't know where to start or what the process entails. We need a roadmap to guide us through common points of interest and past the social terrain and political boundaries that will arise as we journey together and encounter challenging questions like these:

- How do we reconcile with our next-door neighbor?
- How do we reconcile with our coworkers or the folks at church?
- How do we respond to current events?
- How do we hold differing life experiences in tension?
- How do we embrace diversity in our communities?
- How do we reconcile with laborers in other countries who are being paid an unfair wage to make our clothes? Or the aid workers and missionaries abroad who might be doing more harm than good? How do we reconcile with people in India or Pakistan or Russia whom we have never met but whose lives intersect with ours in ways both big and small through our consumerism and social media?

HOW DO WE START?

With over twenty-five years of consulting experience with churches, colleges and organizations, I've been calling people to reconciliation for a long time, but in some ways I've been remiss because I haven't fully explained *how* to go about it. It's like telling your kids that they need to make their own dinner when you've never taught them how to cook! So I've developed a groundbreaking model that I call the Reconciliation Roadmap. Certainly there have been various methods used for reaching harmony before this one, but this approach is a proven process that is based on years of research, practical experience and qualitative data. While I believe it can be applied to all areas of reconciliation, I will focus in this book on the specifics of racial and ethnic reconciliation.

The Reconciliation Roadmap is both individual and systemic. It deals with personal relationships and larger social realities. I've used spiritual, psychological, cultural and social strategies to build this model with a practical framework that will help people participate in God's reconciling work together.

At the end of each chapter you will find a section called "Getting Practical." You will find this book's principles most effective if you use these tools with a group in your organization, church or neighborhood. Whether you're starting with a fresh vision for multiethnicity and need to know where to start, or whether you're already weary from the journey and need encouragement and solutions, this book will be an invaluable resource for you. Let's strive together for more than just a few feel-good moments between people and begin to seek a more sustainable, systemic restoration so that our communities, both local and global, can better reflect the kingdom of God.

This is the book I always wished I had when working in reconciliation. Much of what I learned about leading people in this process was gained through trial and error. Now I want to share the principles I've learned to empower you, the everyday reconciler— the person of God who understands the need for reconciliation and wants to take action. This is also a prophetic call to the church for this time and this unique season. My hope is that this model will illuminate and energize our imagination for what is possible, so together we can create a new reality of reconciliation in communities around the world.

WHAT IS RECONCILIATION?

[Reconciliation] is God's language for a broken world.

Emmanuel Katongole and Chris Rice

||||➤

What exactly is racial reconciliation? If you asked ten different people, it's likely you'd get ten different answers! At a gathering I attended of national multiethnic leaders[1]—pastors, professors, diversity practitioners and leaders of multicultural ministries and denominations—the answer to this question proved quite confusing.

For some, reconciliation meant bringing together a multiethnic group of people who are from similar socioeconomic and educational backgrounds. For others, it meant the pursuit of racial and ethnic diversity but did not include the participation of women in leadership. Still others operated from a model of social empowerment, and for them reconciliation meant that Christians are called to address the discrimination and racism faced by black and Hispanic people in our society.

During the two-day gathering of this elite group, some of whom had written books on the topic of diversity, leaders shared their most poignant beliefs regarding racial reconciliation and best practices for building it. What was most interesting to me, however, was the lack of agreement among the leaders gathered about the term *reconciliation*. There was no single definition or understanding of what reconciliation actually entails.

Do you see the problem? While many of us care about reconciliation and feel called to pursue it as part of our discipleship, there is no clear understanding of what it means to do so! Even among the leading diversity voices of the day there are vastly different beliefs about what it means to pursue reconciliation. Sure, most of us believe that reconciliation means the ending of hostility in order to bring people together, but we still differ, sometimes wildly, in how we believe God calls us to address and engage it.

DEFINING THE TERM

For a while I sought to come up with a new term altogether. I felt that *reconciliation* had perhaps been overused and too often misunderstood. It seems like many people have developed a bias or preconceived notion about what they believe the term means. For example, some people believe *racial reconciliation* is an oxymoron because there has never been a time in American history where racial harmony has existed. One cannot reconcile those who have never enjoyed a conciliatory relationship in the first place. I agree with that, and I fully understand why this term has been disavowed by many, especially when looking at it from a historical and sociological perspective.

Others have a very negative reaction to the word *reconciliation* for a different reason. They feel fear, guilt or shame when they hear the word because of experiences they've had in the past. Meanwhile, some hold the term in a very positive light. For them it denotes a Christian concept, a biblical call for multiethnicity and cultural integration. They eagerly support the process and want people to be challenged to deal with their racism and prejudicial attitudes. However, their notion of the term rarely extends to confronting and changing unjust systems and structures. Moreover, there are those who shy away from the term because it carries the connotation of a "liberal agenda" or the complaints of a vocal minority with no real basis in fact. Whatever the reason, it's challenging to change our thinking and accept a new set of meanings, and I wondered if we might be better off with a new term altogether.

I considered the term *intercultural competence*, but while I could appreciate some of the added clarity it offered, the word *competence* implies that a person can become proficient and the task can be completed. I believe that reconciliation is an ongoing journey, and *intercultural competence* puts an overemphasis on "doing" rather than "being." So I moved on to *cultural credibility* and then later to *intercultural integrity*, hoping to home in on the dynamic interchange between people who are ethnically and culturally different. However, it still lacked something fundamental to my understanding of the term *reconciliation*.

Among those who seek to follow Christ, it is generally understood that in order for reconciliation to occur, there must be repentance, justice and forgiveness. A wrong must be acknowledged and the cause for the lack of unity identified. There is no sustained peace without justice and no sustained relationship without forgiveness. These are crucial in this conversation, yes, but I do not believe that justice and forgiveness alone are enough to produce reconciliation. As with the phrases *intercultural competence* and *intercultural integrity*, something central is still lacking because the church is called to go beyond even this. We are called to go beyond simply making peace or getting enemies to stop fighting—beyond repentance, justice and forgiveness. The Bible invites us further.

Reconciliation is about how to relate even after forgiveness and justice have occurred. It's about how to delve even deeper into relationship with one another. An absence of hostility is possible without a spiritual dimension, but reconciliation is not. Reconciliation is possible only if we approach it primarily as a spiritual process that requires a posture of hope in the reconciling work of

Christ and a commitment from the church to both be and proclaim this type of reconciled community.

REDEFINING THE TERM

With this more complete appreciation and understanding of reconciliation I have come full circle. Since reconciliation is a biblical concept that is rooted in and modeled by the reconciling work of Jesus, I have chosen to reclaim the term instead of replacing it. I want to redeem it and recover its holistic, mysterious and profoundly biblical meaning. It invites us into the bigger story of God's redemptive work in the world. For the purpose of this book and all following conversation, I therefore offer this new definition of the term *reconciliation*:

> *Reconciliation is an ongoing spiritual process involving forgiveness, repentance and justice that restores broken relationships and systems to reflect God's original intention for all creation to flourish.*

This definition acknowledges the historical wounds that must be healed and transcends an individualistic view to include the need for systemic injustice to be addressed as well. However, it is also rooted in a biblical understanding of God, which is why we must take a close look at the theological principles that undergird it.

THEOLOGY MATTERS

Did you know that apartheid in South Africa was based in large part on theological doctrines that were formed at Stellenbosch University in the 1930s and 1940s? Isn't that chilling? Many of the intellectuals at the university took part in the theoretical formulation of Afrikaner nationalism, and the distorted Christian theology that disseminated from Stellenbosch Seminary informed and fueled many Afrikaners' belief that they were God's chosen people. They saw themselves as biologically superior to other races and therefore called to create a new segregated society that would allow them to civilize other people while not tainting themselves with the "darkness and barbarism" of those inferior groups.

These doctrines gave the white South Africans religious justification for *horrific* crimes against their countrymen and women. More than 3.5 million black, Indian and biracial people were removed from their homes in what was one of the largest mass removals in modern history. Nonwhite political representation was obliterated. Black South Africans were denied citizenship and relegated to the slums called "Bantustans." The government segregated education, medical care, beaches and other public services, providing black, Indian and other "colored" people with significantly inferior services. The result was a segregated society where people were dehumanized based on beliefs that were supported by bad theology.

That's why it's crucial that our theology be sound. *Our theology matters!* Those who worked to construct a theological case for apartheid understood that a system of thought cloaked in biblical language would give persuasive force to their segregated system. Our theology informs our anthropology, which in turn informs our sociology. That is to say, what we believe about God will tell us what we believe about people; and what we believe about people will tell us what kinds of communities and societies we believe we should strive to create.

THE CULTURAL MANDATE

So let's press in to our theology of reconciliation. It starts in Genesis 1:28 with what is known as "the cultural mandate," or the command to fill the earth. Here we see that variation was one of God's creational motives from the outset. The creation account reveals God's desire for the earth to be filled with a great diversity of races and peoples.

The first human beings were directed to fill the earth and bring it under the reign of God. To achieve this, people would need to procreate and multiply in number, and this would make it necessary for them to move out and migrate throughout the earth. As this migration took place, these nomads would begin to encounter different types of environmental conditions, and as they adapted to their surroundings, different cultural lifestyles would start to emerge. For example, a group encountering a particular soil condition would need to grow and eat crops that were specific to that particular region's soil and climate. This would require them to develop different farming, hunting and cooking methods.

Migration would also mean that as a group of people encountered weather conditions that were new to them, they would need to adapt, wearing clothes and building houses suitable for their particular environment. So the result of God's command to fill the earth would be *difference*. Different stories. Different words. Different myths, songs, styles of communication, food, clothing . . .

The development of different cultures didn't take God by surprise! This is what the triune God intended from the beginning. Cultural difference and diversity was always a part of God's original plan for human beings. When God commanded the first human beings to "fill the earth," it was a decree to create cultures, because no one culture, people or language can adequately reflect the splendor of God.

THE TOWER OF BABEL

Multiplication and migration are proceeding well until we get to the Tower of Babel in Genesis 11. While this narrative admittedly does not offer enough depth to support a full theology of language and culture, it does provide us with a window into an encounter between the Godhead and humanity in which the nature of each is further revealed. It also provides us a place to do theological inquiry in response to the story of the text. Take a look:

Now the whole earth had one language and the same words. And as they migrated from the east, they came upon a plain in the land of Shinar and settled there. And they said to one another, "Come, let us make bricks, and burn them thoroughly." And they had brick for stone, and bitumen for mortar. Then they said, "Come, let us build ourselves a city, and a tower with its top in the heavens, and let us make a name for ourselves; otherwise we shall be scattered abroad upon the face of the whole earth." The LORD came down to see the city and the tower, which mortals had built. And the LORD said, "Look, they are one people, and they have all one language; and this is only the beginning of what they will do; nothing that they propose to do will now be impossible for them. Come, let us go down, and confuse their language there, so that they will not understand one another's speech." So the LORD scattered them abroad from there over the face of all the earth, and they left off building the city. Therefore it was called Babel, because there the LORD confused the language of all the earth; and from there the LORD scattered them abroad over the face of all the earth. (Genesis 11:1-9)

At first glance, this story may seem to suggest that God is insecure or intimidated by human progress. Or it might be looked upon as a functional story that explains how humankind gained diverse languages. Still others might see the resulting diversity as a punitive curse from God. All of these interpretations, however, would be a superficial understanding of the text, particularly when we read it with the cultural mandate from Genesis 1 in mind.

The kinship group that we encounter in Genesis 11 was refusing to migrate any further. They refused to fill the earth with the *imago Dei*. They chose instead to disregard the diversifying process and hold fast to their homogeneity. They wanted to make a name for themselves, and to think that the Godhead was threatened by this is not consistent with a full understanding of God's character and the original intent for a diverse humanity. To view culture and ethnicity

as simply consequences of sin obscures the larger purpose of God
and distorts the role of diversity in human relationships. God's response to the people's refusal to migrate in Genesis 11 was to confuse
their language and scatter them in order to bring about the divine
will and original purpose for humanity, which is to fill the earth with
the glory of God.

TODAY'S TOWERS

The inclination to build a tower was a metaphorical attempt to in-
stitute a new source of power carved out of human mastery and
imagination. The tower was sort of a totem, a visual symbol that
could reify the formation of a new civilization—an oblique icon of
human superiority. This new civilization would exemplify human
proficiency and efficacy and would rival the world order that God
intended. The threat to the Godhead was both systemic and sym-
bolic, and it continues to this day.

Where do we see this playing out today? Our world is diverse
now, to be sure, but don't we still cling to those who look like us?
Do we not still lean in the direction of sameness and homogeneity?

Look at our churches, where groups of people who look *just* like
each other come together every week.

Look at the way we demand that others speak *our* language and
eat *our* food.

Look at the way we huddle together with those who share our
religious, social and political viewpoints.

Look at the organizational systems and structures we build that
explicitly or implicitly reward those who are like us and exclude,
discriminate or disadvantage those who are not.

These are contemporary examples of how we, like those at the
Tower of Babel, use our human ingenuity, intellect, creativity and
technology to establish structures for ourselves and rebel against
God's plan to bless all people. God resists our empire-building tendency toward homogeneity and causes us to realize our human

limitations. This forces us to recognize our interdependence with others and our need for reconciliation. It challenges us to reengage with the divine, cultural mandate so that all the families of the earth can be blessed. We *need* our differences in order to reflect the glory of God, which is our mission and human calling. This was God's original intent in the beginning, and it is still God's will for the human family today.

FROM BABEL TO PENTECOST

Some scholars, such as Anthony C. Thiselton, believe that the story of Babel is continued in the New Testament book of Acts.[2] Following the death, resurrection and ascension of Jesus, the disciples stayed put in Jerusalem, hiding out. I don't blame them! They stayed right where they were, no doubt in fear that they would meet the same awful fate that befell their leader. So instead of engaging others and mobilizing themselves to spread the good news as Jesus commanded, they sat tight. They waited and they prayed, and they picked new leaders. However, staying put was not a viable long-term strategy or option. They needed to galvanize themselves and move forward, because as long as they stayed in Jerusalem with their own ethnic group, they could rely on their human skills and abilities. In order to fulfill the Great Commission to make disciples of all nations, they would need to move beyond the shelter of their own people, and this would require a power much greater than their personal abilities. They would need to receive the Holy Spirit.

The outpouring of the Holy Spirit on the day of Pentecost signaled the dramatic entry of a new age in human history. Although not the fullness of the kingdom, it was a sign of the kingdom, and it was the empowering of humanity to surrender to the design of God. It was the reception of the Holy Spirit that first offered the church hope of a social and spiritual community composed of people from "every tribe and nation" and unified by the centrality of Christ.

Babel and Pentecost, therefore, provide different examples of a human response to God's command. At Pentecost once again, God came down in response to human behavior and there was confusion. However, this time instead of having a scattering effect, the diverse languages served to bring people together. Through Christ and the Spirit, the walls of separation were brought down. One new humanity has begun.

MOVING THE MANDATE FORWARD

The lesson learned by the disciples at Pentecost applies to us as well. We *cannot* accomplish God's mission in our own ability or strength. If we are to move out beyond the safe and familiar surroundings of our own ethnic groups in order that the church might better reflect the image of God by including people from every tribe and nation, we will need the Spirit of God to empower us.

I pray for the power and the blessing of the Holy Spirit to be upon *you* as you seek to be a part of a community of reconciled people. And I pray for the Holy Spirit to be upon the church as we strive together to live out the meaning of reconciliation and fulfill the mandate to completely fill the earth with the awe-inspiring image of God.

⫸ GETTING PRACTICAL

Look up and read aloud the following passages. Choose three of these key passages that provide insight that can help us develop a biblical perspective on diversity.

Genesis 1:27

Numbers 15:15

Isaiah 11:6-9

Matthew 28:18-20

Acts 10:15-16

Acts 10:34-35

Revelation 5:9

Revelation 7:9

Using the biblical passages above, in a sentence or two write your own definition of reconciliation from a biblical point of view.

- Share it with one other person. What would you like to add or change?

- Call out key elements of your definition for all to hear, and then draft a common definition as a group.

Read the following excerpt from the Belhar Confession, which a sister church in South Africa adopted in 1986.[3] Circle anything you see that is relevant for your group in particular.

We believe in one holy, universal Christian church, the communion of saints called from the entire human family.

We believe

- that Christ's work of reconciliation is made manifest in the Church as the community of believers who have been reconciled with God and with one another;

- that unity is, therefore, both a gift and an obligation for the Church of Jesus Christ;

- that through the working of God's Spirit it is a binding force, yet simultaneously a reality which must be earnestly pursued and sought: one which the people of God must continually be built up to attain; that this unity must become visible so that the world may believe that separation, enmity and hatred between people and groups is sin which Christ has already conquered, and accordingly that anything which threatens this unity may have no place in the Church and must be resisted;

- that this unity of the people of God must be manifested and be active in a variety of ways: in that we love one another; that we experience, practice and pursue community with

one another; that we are obligated to give ourselves will-
ingly and joyfully to be of benefit and blessing to one another; that we share one faith, have one calling, are of one
soul and one mind; have one God and Father, are filled with
one Spirit, are baptized with one baptism, eat of one bread
and drink of one cup, confess one Name, are obedient to
one Lord, work for one cause, and share one hope; together
come to know the height and the breadth and the depth of
the love of Christ; together are built up to the stature of
Christ, to the new humanity; together know and bear one
another's burdens, thereby fulfilling the law of Christ that
we need one another and upbuild one another, admon-
ishing and comforting one another; that we suffer with one
another for the sake of righteousness; pray together; together serve God in this world; and together fight against
all which may threaten or hinder this unity;

- that this unity can be established only in freedom and not
  under constraint; that the variety of spiritual gifts, opportunities, backgrounds, convictions, as well as the various
  languages and cultures, are by virtue of the reconciliation
  in Christ, opportunities for mutual service and enrichment
  within the one visible people of God;

- that true faith in Jesus Christ is the only condition for
  membership of this church;

Therefore, we reject any doctrine

- which absolutizes either natural diversity or the sinful separation of people in such a way that this absolutization
  hinders or breaks the visible and active unity of the church,
  or even leads to the establishment of a separate church formation;

- which professes that this spiritual unity is truly being main-
  tained in the bond of peace while believers of the same

confession are in effect alienated from one another for the sake of diversity and in despair of reconciliation;

- which denies that a refusal earnestly to pursue this visible unity as a priceless gift is sin;

- which explicitly or implicitly maintains that descent or any other human or social factor should be a consideration in determining membership of the church.

How might you bring this confession into the life of your church or group?

2

LANDMARKS OF RECONCILIATION

Lament, repentance, reconciliation and justice are not peripheral to the gospel but intrinsic to it.

Mark DeYmaz

I used to belong to a church that no longer exists. We were founded on a vision of being a multicultural worshiping congregation that was empowered by the Holy Spirit to do innovative outreach in the community. For me it was a dream come true. However, after I had been a member of this thriving church for twelve years, it folded. It's hard to pinpoint the ultimate reason for our demise, but as I look back on it, we couldn't successfully navigate the complexities of creating a diverse culture to facilitate lasting change. Our leadership was not equipped to help move people out of old patterns and did not empower others to deal honestly with the need for healthy systems where issues of trust could be adequately addressed.

Many churches and organizations *want* to promote and facilitate racial reconciliation, but most make very little progress in actually changing the intrinsic culture of their group. By examining the theology, sociology, psychology and organizational change theory involved in reconciliation, I discovered that a journey with landmarks and distinctive phases is the best way to think about the reconciliation process. This is what will help churches and organizations and communities actually move themselves forward in the reconciliation process. Transformation is rarely linear. It's usually more of a winding process. Understanding this is the crucial first step in the Reconciliation Roadmap.

BREAKING GROUND

I began the process of analyzing and explaining the reconciliation process when I was a doctoral student. My goal was to develop a viable model based on my years of experience with racial and gender reconciliation as a consultant to churches, Christian colleges and organizations. It wasn't enough, though, to simply document the many personal and professional experiences reported by my students and other participants in the diversity trainings I facilitated. Nor was it enough to generate a theory that captured my *ideas* of reconciliation if they could not be duplicated or implemented in other contexts.

It was crucial to develop a process that was rooted in solid principles of individual and systemic change. Therefore, undergirded by the theological urgency established in the previous chapter, the first conceptual brick of the model came from social psychology. In the midst of my studies I came across a theoretical framework known as Contact Theory, which suggests that relationships between conflicting groups will improve if they have meaningful contact with one another over an extended period of time.[1] This contact must occur in a *mutually* beneficial learning environment and involve multiple opportunities for the participants to have cooperative interactions with one another. According to the theory, this type of contact will likely decrease the hostility between groups because the animosity is typically fueled by stereotypes that result from limited exposure.

Contact Theory proposes that if diverse groups spend extended time together, their intergroup conflict and the negative effects of racism and ethnocentrism will gradually decrease and possibly even disappear altogether. A theoretical way to explain what many of my students, clients and colleagues had experienced over the years as they engaged with one another in extended positive contact was *exactly* what I had been looking for! Contact Theory was the key that unlocked the conceptual door of the Reconciliation Roadmap.

After I established Contact Theory as my theoretical foundation, the model continued to evolve, and my focus shifted toward practical application. When I was working as a consultant and developing my own curriculum for training, I identified specific characteristics and skills that indicate whether a person or group is actively engaged in reconciliation. Not all people have the same social skills and motivation to cross vast racial and ethnic barriers, regardless of any moral concern they might express. Valuing reconciliation is *not* the same as actively engaging in a process that requires commitment and sacrifice. I understood the need for people to interact in positive ways for an extended period, but I wondered how I might actually motivate people to do it!

Then I was introduced to Benjamin Bloom's taxonomy: an ordering of learning objectives within education. In Bloom's classification system, learning at a higher level is dependent on having attained prerequisite knowledge and skills at a lower level. As these skills are achieved, the taxonomy clearly describes what the learner should be able to do as a result of having acquired certain skills. I applied this taxonomy to the Reconciliation Roadmap as a means of motivation and a rubric for development. Here are the key objectives this taxonomy helped me address:

- describing what a reconciler should be able to know, feel and do as a result of progressing through each stage of the model

- listing the specific skills or metaskills that a person must develop in order to become an effective agent of reconciliation

- naming the specific landmarks and clarifying the intended goal of each one
- identifying what people need to learn before moving on to the next phase

Early on this model was conceptually grounded in social psychology and educational theory and focused on individual learning rather than group or organizational change. That was not enough. I want to teach people how to be reconcilers, yes, but I also want to train them to build *communities* of reconciliation. It's not enough to build a model for individual change if we ignore the groups that shaped them and the communities in which they live. Cultural transformation in a church or organization *must* go beyond interpersonal models of changing "one person at a time," which dominates Western evangelical thinking. The goals of reconciliation need to shift from interpersonal acceptance to building reconciling communities of racial, ethnic, class and gender diversity.

People around the world are experiencing *significantly* different types of conflict, however, and therefore their approach to reconciliation will necessarily differ. For example, some people are living in sites of "hot conflict." When there is shooting, bombing, raping and genocide, there isn't time or space or capacity for discussing a reconciliation model! Instead, with "hot conflict" the emphasis must be primarily on ending the violence and finding ways to mediate the immediate conflict and facilitate some stable boundaries to negotiate peace.

"Cold conflict," on the other hand, is an indirect ongoing ideological confrontation that does not offer hope of peace or honor for those who engage in it. The absence of direct and active violence in zones of cold conflict can lead to the assumption that there *is* no antagonism there. However, chronic inequality and devaluation of people groups engender a strife that hovers just beneath the surface, and we often see it erupt over even the slightest provocation. There are *many* instances in the United States of racially charged aggression, gender inequity and systemic injustice, and the majority of these would be characterized as "cold conflict." The strategies necessary to bridge the racial, religious, gender, tribal and cultural divides of cold conflict can be difficult to grasp. It is for these spaces and places of cold conflict that I offer the Reconciliation Roadmap as a guide.

DEFINING THE LANDMARKS

I have identified five primary landmarks as signs of progress that will produce lasting personal and cultural change in people and groups who seek to live out the biblical vision of reconciliation together as a diverse community:

- catalytic events
- realization
- identification
- preparation
- activation

Catalytic events are vital in the reconciliation process, as they are the primary vehicles for moving people out of old patterns, assumptions and perceptions and into transformative cycles of change. The other landmarks focus on the attitudes, knowledge and skills necessary to grow and achieve authentic and lasting reconciliation.

This model is unique in that it goes beyond the historical practices of adding personnel and increasing the number of culturally diverse people in a group (which rarely, if ever, works). Such strategies have not proved effective in transforming the patterns of how people relate to one another. And education and training alone can't do it either. The Reconciliation Roadmap demonstrates the ongoing process necessary to produce systemic change and aims to teach you how to build communities of reconciled people. Take a look at the Roadmap diagram to get a feel for each phase in the model.

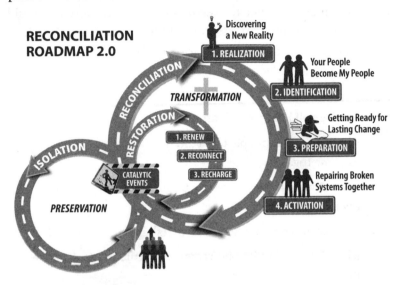

The Reconciliation Roadmap guides the process for reconciling communities with racial, ethnic and other societal differences. It helps individuals *and* groups navigate the arduous path to enduring systemic change. Ongoing interaction in a collaborative environment is inherent in every phase, and a foundational commitment to forgiveness, humility and the pursuit of justice is woven throughout the model.

Now that you have this overview, I invite you to join me on this transformative reconciliation journey. I guarantee that there will be personal and systemic transformation as we engage in this life-changing process of social healing together.

Ⅲ➤ GETTING PRACTICAL

Our racial and ethnic identity is important to God. Without our cultural and ethnic backgrounds we have a limited and incomplete perspective of who God is. Use a puzzle to help your group experience Contact Theory and to illustrate the complexity and difficulty of coming together for reconciliation. This exercise should take about forty-five minutes and will help your group see how we're all interconnected and therefore need each other to complete the work God has called us to do.

Objectives
This exercise will help participants to learn

- what it takes for people from different racial and ethnic groups to come together
- what strategies are necessary to pursue racial and ethnic reconciliation
- why racial reconciliation is so puzzling and confusing
- what the joy of unity and racial reconciliation feels like when we achieve it
- how to move beyond racial segregation to reconciliation

Scripture
Ephesians 2:10-22

Materials Needed

- one puzzle with enough pieces for each person to have one
- flip charts or whiteboard
- colored markers
- table or flat surface large enough to hold assembled puzzle
- Bible

Facilitating the Exercise
Opening

- Give every person a puzzle piece as they walk in.

- Establish ground rules (see "Creating Safe Spaces" in chapter 5).
- Open in prayer and read Scripture: Ephesians 2:10-22.

Phase 1
Using the following questions, ask each person to examine his or her piece of the puzzle:

- What piece of the puzzle do you have?
- What do you know about your piece of the puzzle?
- What does it tell you?
- What do you think it is?
- How do you feel about your puzzle piece?
- Are you one of those who do not like to put puzzles together? Why? What makes it difficult?
- Or are you one who enjoys putting puzzles together? Why?
- What do you want to do with your puzzle piece? Why?

Phase 2
Allow the group to put the puzzle together. Observe group dynamics such as the following:

- Who seems to emerge as the leader(s) of the group?
- Does everyone participate? Why or why not?
- What process do they use to put the puzzle together?
- How do they communicate?
- How do they coordinate their efforts?

(Please note that everything is instructive and can be used in the debriefing process.)

Phase 3
Large-Group Debriefing

- After the puzzle is assembled, have people go back to their seats.

- Use the following questions to debrief the experience and help the group to see how the work of ethnic diversity and racial reconciliation is similar to the work necessary to assemble a puzzle.
- Write their responses to the following questions on the board or flip chart.

  - What do we know now that we didn't know before the puzzle came together?

  - What does this suggest?

  - How did it feel to complete the puzzle?

  - What did it take to put the puzzle together? What did you experience or observe about the process?

  - If our different ethnicities and cultures are compared to a puzzle, why is each piece so important? What happens if one piece is missing?

  - Why is your piece of the puzzle important? What happens to the picture if your piece is missing?

  - In what ways is ethnic diversity like a puzzle?

  - How are the issues of race and ethnicity puzzling to you?

  - What would it take for our ethnic and cultural pieces to come together in this group?

  - What are the obstacles we face in putting our pieces together?

Phase 4

Wrap up the session by having everyone complete the following sentence:

      Today I learned that _____.

3

SHAKE IT UP!

The Power of Catalytic Events

Walk the street with us into history. Get off the sidewalk.

Dolores Huerta

Some years ago, the football coach of an NCAA Division III team at a Christian college decided to shake things up. He was tired of losing game after game, so he changed his recruiting process and started looking for potential players in new places. He intentionally started recruiting players from a predominantly African American high school in the hope that the team might finally break its losing streak. Little did he know how these new recruits would impact both the campus and the larger community!

When these new recruits arrived on campus for the fall term, their presence increased the racial diversity of the school exponentially, and only a few of them proved to be prepared for the academic rigor of college-level study. Further, the coach had failed to inform the rest of the campus community about their arrival, so the faculty and staff were not prepared to welcome and support these new students as they made this major transition to campus life. In short, it was a recipe for disaster!

One night a couple of the new student athletes were walking in the neighborhood around the school, and a resident phoned the police to report two men who looked "suspicious." When the police arrived, the black male students explained that they attended the nearby Christian college, but when the campus security personnel arrived on the scene, they denied that the young men were students. Can you imagine how this made those students feel? They accused campus security and the police of racial profiling.

These types of things continued to occur throughout the year, but the tension really escalated following the close of the football season. The antagonism and distance between the African American students and the other undergraduates on campus was steadily increasing, and one day a white student made a derogatory racial comment to one of the black athletes as he walked down the hall of the dormitory. An argument ensued, which led to a physical fight. The residence life staff managed to break up the fight, but they were ill-equipped to defuse the tension that pervaded the dorm thereafter.

This is what I call a *catalytic event* in the life of that university. This term refers to the often painful but necessary experiences that happen to individuals and organizations and serve to jump-start the reconciliation process. Most of us *need* this type of push to help us start the journey. We need someone or something to push us out of our comfort zones and the isolated social enclaves that keep us alienated from other people and their differing perspectives.

PRESERVATION

These social and cultural enclaves to which we cling are our places of refuge. The world makes sense to us there, and our identity is affirmed when we are in close proximity with those who are most like us and share our values. The other people in our group mirror who we are and socialize us to believe certain things about our-selves and others. We see ourselves reflected there, and the rituals and customs that bond us together make us feel safe and com-fortable. Interestingly, though, we typically don't realize we are in such an enclave until a catalytic event pushes us outside of it, and when that happens, we desperately want back in!

It's normal to want to preserve the spaces and the things that have shaped us, because these help us make sense of the world. We hold fast to the things that make us comfortable. Everybody does this. But when we hold too tightly and refuse to interact with others outside our circle, this is what I call being in a *state of preservation* before the catalytic event pushes into our lives. Both are highlighted in the Reconciliation Roadmap image.

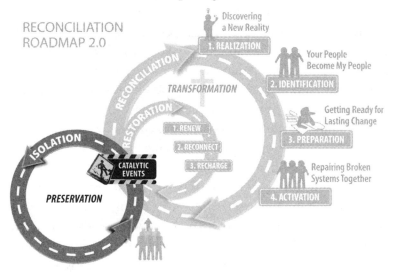

Having been born into specific cultures, ethnic groups and social contexts, most of us begin the reconciliation process in preser-vation and isolation. This is the starting point. As we grow, we try to preserve the values and ways of life that define us, connect us and make us distinctive and special. And unless something happens to move us from this posture of preservation toward including and embracing others, we are prone to *ethnocentrism*. This sociological term denotes belief in the inherent superiority of one's own ethnic group or culture. It also suggests the tendency to consciously or unconsciously view other groups or cultures from the viewpoint of one's own culture and perspective, determining what's "normal," "good or bad," "right or wrong" based on standards that are established by and are most familiar to one's specific ethnic group. This is how we tend to orient ourselves in the world, which is a normal process, but we can quickly become entrenched and inflexible if we culturally isolate ourselves this way.

I remember working with another Christian university that was stuck in preservation. This campus was strongly tied to a conservative church denomination that forbade any expression of charismatic gifts, exuberance in worship and women in leadership. These restrictions extended to a prohibition against associating with anyone who attended a church that allowed such practices—even if they were one's own family members! Everyone was expected to sign a statement of faith that clearly outlined these prohibitions, and anyone who disobeyed was reprimanded.

One administrator at the college was concerned about the lack of diversity on his campus, so he hired me to assess the issues and propose a process that would hew to the denominational restrictions but still help to create a more welcoming environment for students, staff and faculty of color. After we worked at it for a while, however, it became obvious that the ethos of this school was somewhat restrictive. Any cultural expression that departed from the school's white conservative practice of Christianity was severely frowned upon. Although we tried to honor the theological belief system of this university, any changes to the status quo were perceived as threatening—and eventually this fine Christian administrator was fired from his job.

This story illustrates the importance of recognizing that things might have to change if they are to get better. Neutrality is a myth when it comes to reconciliation. The pull of our human tendencies toward self-focus and preservation is too strong and ultimately, albeit often slowly, draws us away from the refining process of becoming reconcilers. At some point we must venture out into the larger world and embrace new ideas. It's inevitable, really. We can't forever avoid contact with people who are unlike us. In most cases such encounters begin to happen when young people go to college, enlist in the military, travel or enter the workforce. This is when assumptions and beliefs that were previously held are often challenged and tested. This is when our view of reality is threatened and the foundational way of seeing our lives is shaken. This is when we are ripe for a "catalytic event." This is the first landmark on our roadmap.

EXPLORING CATALYTIC EVENTS

An example of how catalytic events shake us up and push us into a new reality happened to Captain Chuck Yeager on November 14, 1947. On that day he did something that had never been done before—he broke through the sound barrier! Until then, no aircraft had reached and exceeded the speed of Mach 1. The force exerted on the plane and the human body was so intense at higher speeds that nothing and no one had ever withstood it. Many excellent pilots attempted the feat before Yeager and were tragically killed in the pursuit.

There isn't a doubt in my mind that Yeager was scared. He had to find the depths of his courage and resolve in order to keep pushing forward instead of pulling back. When he broke the sound barrier, Yeager reports, he discovered a new reality of peace and tranquility on the other side.

This is what catalytic events have the potential to do for us. Catalytic events allow us to move from the isolation and stagnation of life in homogeneous groups and break through into a new reality that introduces us to something we have never experienced before.

John Paul Lederach, a Mennonite scholar and peace practitioner, refers to catalytic events as "turning points." He suggests that they are unexpected moments when new life is infused into the "barren" space of a conflict situation and that these unexpected moments make it possible for constructive change to take place. "Constructive change" sounds encouraging, but catalytic events and turning points are *not* moments of clarity. They are not clear-cut and easy. Often they cause us to experience real confusion and angst.[1]

Many of us are interested in talking about strategies for reconciliation, and that's good. But we need to realize that the most powerful ways we change are often out of our control. Change can be painful and coercive because we cannot control or manage it. Conversion and comprehensive change is arduous, difficult and often *very* slow, because it requires us to give up long-held beliefs and assumptions. That's why it often takes a catalytic event in our lives to *force* us out of our spaces of comfort and into new spaces of growth and transformation.

The word *catalyst* comes from the Greek words *katalysis* and *katalyein*, which literally mean "to dissolve" and "loosen." Considering these terms scientifically, if we want to bring about the chemical reaction required for dissolution, it is necessary to decrease or "loosen" the strength of a chemical bond, or to increase the energy to overcome that bond. As many of us likely recall from high school science classes, a catalyst can work by altering the activation energy of a reaction or the amount of energy needed for a reaction. It agitates the atoms, encouraging them to "bump" into each other more often and thus to form new molecular arrangements or relationships. Catalysts can also lower the level of resistance needed for activation so that a change can occur more quickly.

A catalyst is used to initiate or increase the rate of a chemical reaction but is not consumed or altered by the chemical reaction itself. Thus a catalyst can often be reused over and over again in subsequent chemical reactions. In a high school lab experiment the catalyst is typically the last thing added, the significant ingredient needed for any reaction to occur. Without the help of a catalyst, chemical reactions might never occur; then there can be no new arrangement of molecules. Or the reaction process would take much longer.

Of course transformational change on the communal and personal level is *much* more difficult to control than a chemical reaction. The outcomes can be so much harder to predict, and the number of possibilities is much greater in human systems than in those that govern the outcome of mixing chemical compounds. Still, there are helpful parallels we can draw between chemical catalysts and reconciliation to help us understand the process.

When engaging in the work of reconciliation, we must increase our openness and decrease our resistance to change. Just as in our high school lab experiments in which the key chemicals are present but unable to activate without the catalyst, we need a catalyst. Even when there is significant *desire* for peace and reconciliation, it's incredibly challenging to change our entrenched cycles in order to allow for the possibility of new relationships. We are so accustomed to our own social circles and homogeneous units. We truly don't know any other way! So we need a catalyst to shake us up, lower our resistance and push us out and into the space God envisions for us.

A CATALYTIC CONVERSION

Saul's conversion in Acts 9 is a perfect example of a catalytic event. He was on his way to Damascus, where he planned to escort followers of Jesus back to Jerusalem, coercively repatriating them. Saul's desire to protect the purity and authority of Jewish law had led him to see both Jesus and his followers as his enemies. And Saul of Tarsus was *certain* he was right.

On the road, however, Saul encountered a great heavenly light that knocked him to the ground, and he heard the voice of God. In the process he was blinded. He was told to continue on to

Damascus, but he wasn't told whether he would ever regain his sight. Moreover, he didn't know how he would manage to reconstruct his life.

Can you picture yourself in Saul's shoes? Can you imagine what it would be like to wait in literal and figurative darkness? Do you identify with his anguish? Because we know the story's outcome, the distress of Saul's catalytic event and subsequent wait in Damascus may not seem like a big deal to us. But we shouldn't gloss over the discomfort, even agony, that he must have suffered at this time of immense transformation.

It is in the confusion of this darkness that Saul's conversion begins, as his former certainties collapse and he is forced to open up to new things. For Saul turned Paul, his catalytic event pushed him into a new realm of vulnerability and opened him to the possibility of change. His blindness brought him to a place where he was eventually able to see anew!

That's what catalytic events are supposed to do. They force a shift. They push us out of our old framework and into a new way of seeing. This is both cognitive and affective, and it can be incredibly disruptive to the status quo, as we saw in the case of Paul. The old does not fit into the new, and life no longer makes sense in the same way. Catalytic events can be confusing and deeply disorienting. This will be true in our pursuit of reconciliation, and we must learn to see the confusion and discomfort as part of the change process that will eventually move us toward transformation.

We know that stress and distress are both producers and products of change, but it's also helpful to understand *how* our brains change and the role external events play in the process. Bruce Wexler, a neuroscientist and psychiatrist, tells us how our brains process change in his book *Brain and Culture*.[2] His study of the brain's neuroplasticity offers us an important look at the role social culture plays in the neurobiological formation of the brain. Wexler's research suggests that we are prone to resist change. It is part of the way we are wired. We have a tendency to deny information that conflicts with our beliefs, and we will therefore shape new information to fit our preexisting ideas.

This is so important for us to understand. Many of our attempts at reconciliation fail because we are not taking account of the psychological and cultural resistance that people bring to the process. *This* is precisely why sustained reconciliation is so hard! But as leaders who want to influence others to embrace the reconciliation process, we need to know how to move past this resistance to change. We need to find a way to push people beyond their propensity to preserve their current ways of thinking and energize them to move in an entirely new direction. We've got a hard row to hoe!

Wexler explains that the developing human brain shapes itself to the cultural environment.[3] As a result, our outside world becomes the orientation for our inside world. Wexler calls this inner-outer world congruence the "principle of internal-external consonance."[4] Repeated brain activities in response to the same external events establish a pattern or cycle of responses. Moreover, as we age, our brains lose some of their ability to adapt to new stimuli with different patterns of response.

Consequently we become more resistant to change. We resist changing our inner responses to reflect the changing outer world, and we become more invested in preserving consonance. This means we work even harder to make the outside world fit our inside world and to shape our cultural environment to fit what makes us feel more congruent. And we do all of this without even realizing it!

When we experience a catalytic event, the new stimuli can overwhelm us and create a sense of dissonance and distress. Our brains work very hard to fit the new data with the patterns we've always held as good and true. But when the catalyst is sufficiently unnerving, it can force us to rework old ideas and former frameworks in order to manage the new stimuli.

CHICAGO URBAN PROJECT

Years ago I facilitated an internship program with InterVarsity Christian Fellowship designed to provide Christian community development and urban ministry training for college students. For an entire summer, students from sundry racial, ethnic, socioeconomic and political backgrounds lived together in Chicago. They worked as camp counselors and tutors for inner-city children, and they had to shop, cook, eat, work and worship in the neighborhood they served.

During the first week of the program I administered a pretest to establish a baseline for the group's attitudes, knowledge and skills in regard to race, ethnicity and gender. All the students already valued cultural diversity and gender equality highly, and they all strove to be on their best "diversity behavior." They used inclusive language and refused to tolerate any hint of racism. I remember one young woman who was very proud of the fact that she was the only white female in the gospel choir at her school. All of these students, in their own estimation, had already been reconciled.

Although this was impressive to my staff and me, we could see that it was ultimately superficial and we would need to dig a little deeper. So midway through the program, in an attempt to help them press further in, we took the group through an experiential learning exercise called the Race Reversal Fantasy. Little did we know that this exercise would prove to be a catalytic event for the group and nearly destroy the group altogether! The students were instructed to imagine themselves as a member of the racial group that they were least comfortable with. As they visualized this, they were guided through a typical day and asked to envision themselves in the life of a person from the racial group they had chosen. As they progressed through their imaginary day they were asked to notice what their physical features were like, what foods they ate, how they spent their time, where they lived and what their family life was like.

After the guided imagery was over, the students were given 3×5 cards and asked to answer questions based on their recollections of the experience. Their responses were anonymous, and we posted them around the room for the group to mull over. The stereotypical nature of many of the reflections caused quite a stir. Many of the students felt hurt, angry, bitter and betrayed. After reading one of the responses, a black female student turned to face the group and shouted, "Who said this?" Everyone in the room froze.

The tension was palpable. One Korean student actually called her father and asked him to come get her. Some of the African American students from the community refused to spend another night with the team and went home. And several of the white students accused me of being racist myself, charging that I had chosen an exercise that was biased and unfair. It was a mess, and I went home in tears, convinced I had ruined the program and lost the respect of my students.

EMBRACE THE CHAOS

What I discovered that summer with the Chicago Urban Project was that this sort of disruption is an absolutely vital part of the reconciliation process. It's important to be aware, however, that there are major power and safety dynamics that come into play when there is chaos. People need to know who is in charge and who will keep them safe. It's a risky part of the process because people can be seriously hurt and they might want to get out altogether. *I* certainly experienced my share of anxiety with our group that summer! I was ready to throw in the towel. But then I remembered that distress is *needed* to overcome the resistance we naturally have to forming new relational patterns.

Edgar Schein, an organizational change specialist, posits that groups and organizations resist learning new patterns because it creates anxiety, and I think he is absolutely right. Schein points out the inherent paradox when he says, "Anxiety inhibits learning, but anxiety is also necessary if learning is going to happen at all."[5] Our group needed to be shaken up! It was necessary, and we pushed through to new and unexplored territory as a team because of it.

Chaos is a necessary stage in the community-building process. It won't last forever, but we can't skip this part no matter how much we might like to pass over it. Chaos is counterintuitive and problematic because our human nature craves equilibrium and a sense of stability. This is normal. However, we can value equilibrium too highly. Human beings actually *need* disorder and a sense of disequilibrium in order to grow and change. We need chaos in order for transformation to take place. There is no new life without the disruption of chaos. In fact, it is the heart of the Christian faith to believe that life comes from death.

The particularly difficult piece is figuring out where to go with our anxiety and sense of disorientation. What's next? Schein says that the key lies in our "ability to balance the amount of threat produced by disconfirming data with enough psychological safety to allow [us] to accept the information, feel the anxiety and become motivated to change."[6] If a catalytic event occurs when there is little sense of safety, individuals and groups can experience a form of trauma that shuts down their creative capacity, and they will revert to a place of alienation and preservation.

Transformation requires disruption and a degree of chaos to increase the sense of urgency that change *must* happen. However, there must also be enough psychological safety that the chaos does not completely overwhelm our ability to reflect and reorganize ourselves. A catalytic event will either push us forward toward transformation or tighten our tether to preservation. In my work as a consultant I have seen strategies that were stressful enough to create change but ultimately were not safe enough to allow people to form new patterns. On the other hand, I've also seen educational strategies that allowed safe spaces for open dialogue but did not create enough discomfort to push a group's members beyond their old patterns of relating. There must be both!

The Chicago Urban Project students had hit a crucial point in their path to real community. Prior to the Race Reversal Fantasy exercise, the group was in what M. Scott Peck calls the "pseudo-community" stage. In his book *The Different Drum: Community Making and Peace*,[7] he explains that most groups begin with a safe level of interaction. The members rarely argue or disagree with each other, and relationships are characterized by friendliness, tolerance and great care not to offend one another. That's exactly where we were before the Race Reversal exercise! However, in order to move to a deeper and more genuine level of relating, our group had to experience chaos by expressing our differences and seeing each other's imperfections.

The question now was whether they had the ability to go forward and experience genuine community or would choose to bail. Was it safe enough to move forward?

I called the group together the following day to regroup and debrief the exercise. I explained that what had happened the previous day was a good thing. Instead of seeing it as a catastrophe, I reframed it for my students as a catalytic event. I explained the disruption and the chaos, clarified what had happened and gave it meaning. Now we could enter the *emptying* stage that follows chaos to produce constructive change. This is when each person "empties" himself or herself of the need to change or persuade anyone else. So we shared our thoughts, feelings and opinions as a way to disclose our true selves. As each person risked this type of vulnerability, the group listened without passing judgment, seeking mutual understanding and respect. It was a long conversation, but ultimately the previous day proved to be a powerful catalytic event for the group. The students and I were revitalized to continue in our reconciliation journey and enter the realization phase.

So, you see, if we endure the shakeup we can experience true community with a new level of honesty and transparency that leads to personal transformation and social change. Catalytic events can

be painful and disruptive, but they can also be harnessed for good
to move us forward into reconciliation.

▥➤ GETTING PRACTICAL

Have you ever experienced a catalytic event? What happened?

- Did this catalytic event affect a group of people or you as an individual?

- How did you or your group respond?

- Why do you think you or your group responded in that particular way?

- Do you think you would respond differently to the same catalytic event if you were given the chance again? Why or why not?

Using the day of Pentecost in Acts 2:1-21 as an example of a multiethnic catalytic event, notice what has happened in your community or organization to cause the following to occur:

- get your attention

- cause fear, panic and confusion

- force new questions

- provide new opportunities for the gospel to be proclaimed

- move you toward preservation or transformation

As a reconciler like the apostle Peter, how can you and your group participate in helping to

- *identify* what God is doing?

- *interpret* and give meaning to these events from a kingdom perspective?

- *integrate* changes into everyday life and ministry to sustain the impact of the event?

4

A SHIFT IN PERSPECTIVE

The Realization Phase

I am working for a world in which diversity is seen as a source of celebration rather than a cause for alarm.

Toni Morrison

||||➡

Brock Schroeder used to teach astronomy at Olivet Nazarene University in Illinois, and he prided himself on being open to exploring a wide range of perspectives in his life and work. In the natural sciences, though, it's typically understood that physical laws are the same regardless of one's personal background. A focus on learning such things as the order of the planets and the scale of the universe should then mean that all of Dr. Schroeder's students wind up with the same knowledge from taking his classes.

One semester, though, Schroeder was with his class in the planetarium, and he was demonstrating how one's latitude on Earth determines one's view of the sky. The position of the sun, moon and stars in the sky is different depending on where one is located on the Earth. One student in his class was from Argentina, so to illustrate his point, Schroeder decided to simulate what the sky would look like that night in Buenos Aires. As he manipulated the controls to set up the projector to show the Argentinian sky, however, he experienced something disorienting. Many of the constellations with which he and his North American students were familiar appeared very different, and some did not appear at all. Of course he had known from an intellectual standpoint that this would be so, but he had experienced it so rarely that it unnerved him. He felt lost in his own planetarium!

Schroeder also noticed that the stars in the part of the sky directly above the South Pole were missing. Upon inspection, he discovered that the company that had built the projector had attached the star ball to its base in such a way as to obscure those particular stars. It was a star projector built by a North American company for North American people. He was flabbergasted. The sky he had been teaching to his students as scientific fact was *not* the same sky that his student from Argentina had seen from his country and his perspective south of the equator.

Schroeder realized in that moment how important it is to seek out other perspectives. You have to be intentional, thoughtful and deliberate if you want to see things from someone else's vantage point. He could have gone the rest of his career not knowing just how different the sky looks from other places in the world, because he had never taken the time to look. What an unexpected gift he received that day! He went on to renovate the planetarium and install a new projector to correct the previous problem, and, more important, he discovered that we have to *choose* to change our viewpoint if we truly want to see things from a different perspective than our own.

THE REALIZATION PHASE

The realization phase of the journey involves more than cognitive understanding. It is more than awareness for the sake of awareness. In this phase we reach beyond vague understanding and intellectual assent and come to an awareness that is *contextually connected.*

This understanding of reality, and a sense of our own relatedness *to* that reality, leads us to own the truth, and the impact of it, for ourselves. In short, it's a state of awareness that *requires a response* because it literally changes everything we thought we understood about an experience. Professor Schroeder was *aware* that the sky looked different depending on his location, but that was as far as it went until that day in the planetarium when he realized what a different perspective would *feel* like and how he had failed his students up to that point.

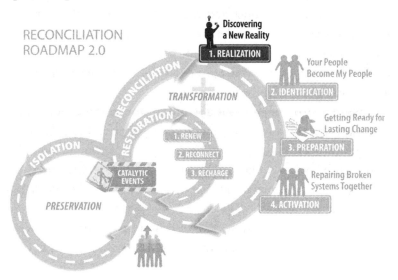

Another example might be a person's discovery that not all homeless people are uneducated and unwilling to work. This seemingly small realization can help them begin to understand and acknowledge some of the other factors that might be at play—unequal educational opportunities, disparity in treatment by police and the courts, concentrated poverty among many minorities, and the like. Realization is more than intellectual awareness or cognitive understanding. It is the *visceral* awareness of reality and a sense of one's relatedness to it.

In order to do this, one must engage in the three essential tasks of the realization phase:

- reorientation
- readiness
- restoration

REORIENTATION

To move into the new realm of possibility that is becoming apparent at this landmark, we must first reorient ourselves. This happens most often following a catalytic event. If this critical incident has indeed opened us up to the possibility that not all of "those people" are bad, say, then we realize our need to rethink and reorient how we see ourselves and how we see others.

I heard a story once about a white pastor in the Chicago area who experienced something genuinely disruptive when he was a young pastor. He had been roughhousing with a young man in his youth group who is black, and while they were wrestling and goofing around, he managed to get the student into a headlock. But rather than relish the victory, he immediately released his student, shouted his name and threw his hands up into the air. The student ran to his aid, thinking he might have hurt him somehow, but the pastor just said quietly, "Your hair is soft."

The teenager touched his head and looked back at him. "Yeah."

They looked at each other for a long moment until the white pastor said, "Do you know what I was told about black people? Do you know what I've always thought? I was told that all black people have hair like steel wool. But—but your hair is *soft*."

The young pastor realized in that moment that what he had been told *all* his life was wrong. The realization came because he had had an undeniable encounter with reality. As a result, he now had to examine what else he had been told about others and himself that might also be untrue. *This* is the hard work of the realization phase.

It requires us to grapple with facts in a way that makes us acknowledge that we and our people have played a part in the problem. We have to *reorient* ourselves.

To do this type of reorientation requires the management of memory. We typically get hooked or stuck on things that have happened to us or to people we have known. Holding on to a history of past wounds can trigger an immediate reactive response of fight or flight whenever we encounter someone or something that reminds us of those memories. To move beyond this sort of unthinking reaction, we must do the hard work of managing and reconsidering these feelings and assumptions so that we can be open to a new way of relating.

READINESS

This second task helps create a fertile environment for reconciliation to take hold. Readiness is what ensues when we identify what is happening in our context, what historical factors still have influence and what resources and capacities are present to make change possible.

For such readiness to come about, the following things are necessary:

- The person or group must see a need for change. It has to be more advantageous to make peace than to make war. At the very least, the leaders involved must see the need for change and be willing to address that need.

- The person or group must see the benefit of change. We must see that change is in our best self-interest. This has to be more than a moral platitude. In order for a new community to thrive, the people involved must see reconciliation as their best choice, or it won't be sustainable long term.

- The person or group must take stock. Do we have the resources, desire, training, capacity, proper conditions, political will, stamina and so on to pursue this new way of being? These things must be present if we are to succeed.

These things might seem obvious—rudimentary even. Further, sometimes we make the mistake of thinking that the realization phase is something we walk through solely as individuals. As long as *I* see the need and the benefit of changing, I'm all set! More often than not, though, change needs to happen within an existing group, and that can be a much more arduous process. We'd be remiss if we underestimated just how onerous and painful it can be to change. Anne Lamott says this in her book *Help, Thanks, Wow* about why change is so important and what makes us so reluctant to engage in it:

> If we stay where we are, where we're stuck, where we're comfortable and safe, we die there. . . . If you want to know only what you already know, you're dying. . . .
>
> When nothing new can get in, that's death. When oxygen can't find a way in, you die. But new is scary, and new can be disappointing, and confusing—we had this all figured out, and now we don't.[1]

RESTORATION

The final task in this phase is restoration, and it is when we begin to identify things to do. There has to be some activity that helps us to return to the hope of possibility. Prior to restoration we often feel as if reconciliation is hopeless; we feel helpless in the face of all the evil and injustice of which we are now painfully aware. When we name things that we can do, it feels like there is possibility within ourselves once more.

Here are examples of things we might do:

- lament by accurately naming the situation and bringing our anger and frustration to God

- take a prayer walk around our community and ask to see signs of God's work and presence already abiding there
- attend an event or rally to learn more and meet other concerned people
- use social media to join a cause, stay informed and stand in solidarity with others
- volunteer and use our time and expertise to serve and interact with people in need
- host a movie night or book club to bring neighbors together in a safe space to talk and share ideas
- prepare a meal for international students so as to learn about one another
- write a letter to the editor of the local newspaper to speak out on a specific issue

Really the options are endless. It only takes some thought and intentionality to figure out what might be a best fit and practice for you. It's vital in the task of restoration, however, that we experience enough safety to open ourselves to one another and allow hope to penetrate the dark places between us. To create such safety, the threat level must be lowered and there must be a commitment to civility. Reconciliation is not possible without these safe spaces— we'll delve into that further at the next landmark.

In order to foster such spaces, we must first acknowledge and validate the wrongs that have taken place between us. This enables us to move away from the limiting roles of oppressor versus oppressed, victimizer versus victim. It also gives people a vision of a nonhostile future. We *must* be able to envision something in order to pursue it. Reconciliation must be fueled by a shared vision of what it can look like so that we can grow in our belief that it is indeed possible.

This point was poignantly demonstrated in a story I heard one night while watching the news on television. A young Palestinian boy was playing outside his home with a toy gun. Israeli soldiers standing guard nearby thought the weapon was real and shot and killed the boy. As you can imagine, his family was absolutely distraught and overcome with grief. But instead of continuing the cycle of violence, the boy's father chose to envision a world where violence could be replaced by peace. So rather than seek revenge, this grieving father decided to donate his son's vital organs to an Israeli hospital to save the lives of seven Jewish children waiting for transplants. It is this type of compassion that allows us to imagine a future world where peace, unity and reconciliation are indeed possible.

This is what Martin Luther King Jr. meant when he said, "If we are to have peace on earth, our loyalties must become ecumenical rather than sectional. Our loyalties must transcend our race, our tribe, our class, and our nation; and this means we must develop a world perspective." As an African American, Dr. King understood that the reconciliation process is vital and beneficial for all of us. People of color find that unique challenges and difficulties come with this call due to our collective history. However, we must persevere for the sake of the gospel. Our participation in the reconciliation process allows our lives to be enriched, our understanding of who we are to be expanded and our worldview to be enlarged because we become able to transcend and break free from the limited ways that society tries to define us.

As I look back over my life, I realize that I am not the same person that I was when I began this reconciliation journey. I've been changed, transformed, by the process. I see the world differently and have a different perspective on who I am in the world. However, most important, I learned that God can use me in ways that I could never have dreamed or imagined. I have become a thought leader with influence and authority in communities around the world. That's huge and I never saw it coming! It's the result of my engagement with intercultural communities, working for reconciliation.

AWARE, SET, GO!

Realization is a state of awareness that requires a response. It creates a readiness for reconciliation because it causes us to realize on a profound level that things *must* change; we cannot stand still. It's the questioning or the partial suspension of the way we previously understood things to be; the suspension of prior meaning frameworks—cultural, relational and personal. It introduces us to new alternatives and choices, and we come to understand that there is more than one way to see things. There are different angles on the same night sky. And the way that we have constructed the world, or the way it was constructed for us, is not necessarily the way the world has to remain. Indeed, there might be something new, something unexplored, that has been waiting for us all along.

Ⅲ▶ GETTING PRACTICAL

Describe an experience when you learned something important about racial and ethnic differences.

- What happened?
- What did you do?
- How did you feel about it?
- What did you learn?

Discuss the following questions with your group:

- Are there people you don't approach because you're afraid you don't know what to talk with them about?
- Are there conversations you don't get into because you don't know how to have the discussion or what to say?
- What makes racial and ethnic issues so hard to talk about?
- What do you fear might happen?

When you are ready to dive in deeper with your group, discuss the following questions:

- Where do you stand on the issue of racial profiling? Do you think people of various races really are singled out and treated differently? Is this practice real, or are some people just hyper-sensitive?

- What do you think about interracial dating? Do you have any issues with it? What do you think are some of the issues that people who date people of a different race have to deal with?

- What is your perspective on the reality of discrimination today? Is this really an issue? Do some people of different races really get different treatment when buying homes, applying for jobs, renting apartments, shopping in stores or buying cars? What do you think are the major issues?

- What is your opinion on affirmative action in educational institutions? Should every person have the same opportunity for a higher education? Should everyone be held to the same educational standards?

- What can be done to get people of different races to come together at the same church? Why do people tend to gravitate toward churches and people that are familiar to them? What are some of the other barriers to a multicultural church?

5

A GROUP EFFORT

The Identification Phase

> *Great achievements are not born from a single vision but from the combination of many distinctive viewpoints. Diversity challenges assumptions, opens minds and unlocks our potential to solve any problem we may face.*

Author Unknown

Over four thousand Christian leaders from 198 countries gathered to address the critical concerns facing the world and the global church at the 2010 Lausanne Congress on World Evangelism in Cape Town, South Africa. The Lausanne movement was started in 1974 by Billy Graham and other prominent evangelical leaders as a way to collaborate and mobilize for world evangelization. One of the hopes for the gathering in Cape Town was to identify the next generation of emerging Christian leaders who would pick up this mandate and carry it forward.

At the congress we grappled with issues of extreme poverty, human trafficking, creation care, world evangelism, HIV/AIDS, immigration and religious pluralism. On the day I spoke, I felt an unexpected urge to publicly state a conviction that was growing stronger and stronger in my heart. I wasn't sure how it would be received, and I felt scared, but I decided to say it anyway. Raising the microphone, I took a deep breath, and the first words out of my mouth were, "I believe that the day of the single superstar is *over*!"

To my great surprise people in the audience roared and clapped their approval. The crowd went nuts! I'm not sure how to explain it, but I got the overwhelming sense that we were all in sync, that in that moment we all understood that the way forward would require cooperation and partnership. Instead of waiting for some great leader like Billy Graham, Nelson Mandela or Mother Teresa to show up and show us how to solve global problems, we would need to unify and collaborate and work *together* for God's good intentions for the world. No one person would lead the way. We would go together.

And so it has been with the 2014 Ferguson protest movement, for example; there isn't a single leader or voice that rises above all the others. It's a *collection* of voices that we are hearing from the streets, on social media and around the world. This is what the *identification* phase is all about.

IDENTIFICATION AND CULTURE

Think back for a moment to the realization milestone. This is when we become aware of our own ethnic identity and the severity of the social problems around us. It's when we acknowledge, perhaps for the very first time, that we are part of the problem. You or your group likely experienced some sort of catalytic event, and it propelled you forward to the realization phase, where you wrestled with your shifting view of the world and your place in it. The identification landmark, on the other hand, is where we begin to identify with and relate to *other* people who are experiencing the same thing. It's where we begin the journey of seeing ourselves as kingdom people and potential reconcilers. It's where we start in on the hard work of building a new collective identity and a collaborative community that can hold the concerns, values, desires and experiences that we share. The identification phase is, therefore, the beginning of shifting our cultural identity.

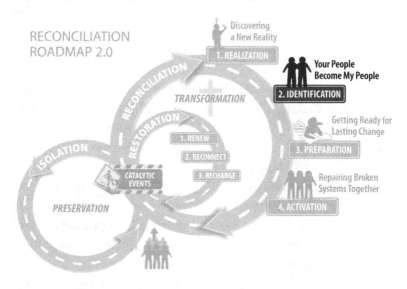

This shift in cultural identity is beautifully depicted in Ruth 1:8-17. Naomi bitterly observes that both her sons and her husband are dead and, at her old age, she will never be able to provide a new husband for either of her widowed daughters-in-law. So Naomi urges Ruth to go back with her sister in-law, who is returning to her own people group. But Ruth refuses to go and says,

Do not press me to leave you
or to turn back from following you!
Where you go, I will go;
where you lodge, I will lodge;
your people shall be my people,
and your God my God.

Ruth's mind was made up. The length of the journey, the dangers and the inevitable fatigue had caused her to identify more deeply with her new family and their culture. She so firmly identified with her mother-in-law that their futures were now inextricably tied together. They related to each other differently because of the painful journey they'd been on together—it had developed a new bond of love between them.

This underscores why it's so important for us to understand that a group is never just a collection of individuals. It also includes a set of explicit or implicit assumptions about how the members of a group should relate to each other. Changing these relational assumptions to allow the space for reconciliation to occur is the primary goal of the identification phase of the journey. Every group everywhere, be it a church or a school, a family or a business, carries with it assumptions about how its members ought to relate to one another. Put simply, every group has its own unique culture. Culture is where individual people and their personal contexts collide with one another. Another way to think of it is as an *ethos*, or the guiding beliefs of your group.

Whether implied or explicit, every group's got an ethos, and usually by the time one observes that a culture or an ethos is lacking in some way, it's so complex and complicated that it's hard to know where to even *begin* to change it. According to entrepreneur Andy Dunn, it's like making mole, a sauce commonly used in Mexican cuisine that can include up to twenty-nine different ingredients.[1] When something is missing, it might taste a little off, but it's going to be hard to pinpoint where things veered off course!

This reminds me of an experience I had while consulting for a Christian college many years ago. I was working with a nearly all-white staff that wanted to increase diversity on the campus but didn't know how. They had been almost completely unsuccessful in hiring a more diverse faculty, *and* they had managed to lose the few professors of color who did work for a time at the school. During the assessment process, they asked me why they were having such a hard time, and I pointed out that their ethos seemed to be very insular. For example, nearly everyone who worked at the college had attended the school as a student or was, at the very least, part of the school's essentially all-white church denomination. They had a shared narrative and a common understanding about who they were. Faculty meetings seemed rather like a family reunion, so that anyone coming from a different denomination or a different educational institution was bound to feel like an outsider. Therefore the campus culture caused any faculty or student of color to feel like they were on the outside looking in at someone else's family reunion! Now it made sense why they never felt at home at the college and ultimately opted not to stay.

Consider a specific group in which you would like to be a reconciler. Is it your school? Your neighborhood? Your church? Your workplace? The identification phase is about working together with the people in this particular group to change the way you interact with one another. The ways that people interact, or the ways they *think* they should interact, usually need to be renegotiated in order for true reconciliation to come about. In other words, the ethos of the group as a whole undergoes transformation during the identification portion of the journey. Automatic perceptions and stereotypes will need to be confronted and worked through, empathy needs room to grow, and mutual understanding must have space to develop.

In order for this to happen, the leaders of the group must recognize the unwritten rules, assumptions and beliefs that shape the culture of the group. If an organization wants to shift its cultural identity, it is crucial that it have an internal team of diverse leaders who model the diversity change initiative. The leaders thus serve as a microcosm of what is hoped for in the broader community. According to John Kotter in his book *Leading Change*,[2] it is typically unrealistic to expect change to occur throughout the entire organi-

zation at exactly the same time. A "guiding coalition" must be empowered to strategically lead the process. When others see positive
results modeled by those leading the process, they are able to envision the possibility of reconciliation for the group. Only then can
change slowly begin to grow and infiltrate the rest of the organization.

This is the transformation process that Jesus Christ calls his followers to step into. He invites us to come and die. In essence he says
that something of our old identity must die and we must now embrace our new identity in him. This is the principle that Jesus talked
about in Matthew 16:25: "For those who want to save their life will
lose it, and those who lose their life for my sake will find it." To be
in relationship with "the other" is to take on a new identity.

My friend Ruth Haley Barton, noted author and founder of the
Transforming Center, explains how our ability to experience transformation is critically connected to our engagement with others
who bring unique and diverse perspectives:

> One of the dynamics of transforming community is that there
> is enough "otherness" in the group that we can actually be
> challenged to stretch and grow beyond the confines of our
> own limited view of things and find ways to open to Christ as
> he is uniquely present in the other. In affinity groups, by con-
> trast, there often isn't enough "otherness" to call forth anything
> new. If we don't venture outside our comfort zones, trusting
> that the stranger God has brought into our lives has something
> for us, we will never even know what we're missing.[3]

Some people may become frightened and perceive the identity
shift as a disloyalty to their original group. But to the contrary, to
participate fully in this process individuals need to have a clear
sense of self on a personal level. This is called *identity security*, and
it is much more than personal identity. It is a sense of connection
with people that you believe are like you. It is also an appreciation
of your own ethnic and cultural heritage that does not lapse into

ethnocentrism. This firmly rooted self-identity allows you to identify and empathize with others without assimilation or having your identity subsumed into another's.

It's also imperative that people have a social awareness that allows them to question their own cultural assumptions and traditions, search for new meaning and purpose, and reclaim aspects of their racial and ethnic heritage to nurture that sense of self. In this new community people should embrace their culture, their ethnicity, their personality and their gender as part of what it means for them to be made in the image of God. And they must encourage the others in the group to do the same. Without this understanding, one cannot progress along the Reconciliation Roadmap. It's foundational to experiencing transformation without losing one's own identity in the process.

CREATING SAFE SPACES

These things won't happen on their own. We have to be intentional within our communities to actually foster these changes and help them take root. Those entering into the identification phase have to understand that the relationships within a group need an interactive peace in order to thrive. In a community where there is conflict or some form of inequality between people who are different, this phase requires collaborative group experiences ensuring that all members can flourish.

To facilitate this, ground rules must be established to ensure that the group is a safe space for all its members. It's vital to the process of reconciliation to create an atmosphere of safety. I use the following ground rules whenever I'm leading a reconciliation process.

Use "I" statements. This enables folks to share their own beliefs and feelings without making dogmatic statements that can alienate others in the group. It also forces people to own their own feelings and beliefs. If members of the group use phrases like "I think that you" or "everybody knows that," others are immediately defensive when they disagree. It's infinitely more effective to say "I feel" or "I think" or "In my opinion."

Don't interrupt. Social Interactions 101. We learn this in grade school, but it's a struggle for adults as well! This second ground rule ensures that people who are speaking are not interrupted in the midst of sharing their thoughts. This is particularly crucial in a large group, where there is bound to be a mix of introverts and extroverts, who process information differently. Extroverts often think out loud and need the time and space to process their thoughts orally in order to come to clarity. On the other hand, introverts tend to process internally, and when they do speak it's important that they are heard and valued for sharing their insights with the group. If not, that introverted person might surmise that their input is not important to the group and retreat into their inner sanctum to continue to process their thoughts. In either case, by not interrupting the speaker, the group is able to demonstrate their respect for one another, which will encourage continued sharing and vulnerability.

Maintain confidentiality. This is perhaps the most important factor in creating a safe environment for growth and change. It allows everyone in the group to trust that they share personal or potentially embarrassing information without fear. It's so important to honor this risk by not discussing what is said with others outside the group. If this ground rule is violated and a person learns that others have talked about what was shared within the group, the consequences can be devastating. Once trust is broken, it is extremely difficult to reestablish; as a result, the group might shut down entirely and refuse to reenter that space of vulnerability.

Be present. This one sounds simple, but it can actually be very hard to accomplish. In this age of smartphones and constant availability through technology, it can be difficult to be fully engaged with one another without distraction. Even when we are physically present with others, our mind and emotional investment may be elsewhere. In order for a reconciled community to be formed, each person must bring their whole self to the process.

Adherence to these kinds of ground rules will allow us to create the atmosphere for trust to be established and a new kind of relating to occur.

BLACK TEARS

Two vital components of the identification landmark are embracing the stories of others and building empathy. Both are crucial for changing perceptions and deobjectifying one another. Someone who was once alien to you must be seen and heard in new ways. It's what the renowned Jewish philosopher Martin Buber calls "I and Thou" relating. Instead of "I-it" relating, where we view others as wholly outside ourselves, distinct and utterly separate, we cross over to "I-Thou" relating, where those boundaries are reconsidered and we begin to belong to each other.

A friend of mine witnessed this shift during a Sankofa Journey, a trip that my church denomination sponsors every year. *Sankofa*, from the Akan language of Ghana, translates in English as "to reach back and get it." The symbol of a bird with its head turned backward taking an egg off its back is often used to illustrate the concept. The word is also associated with an African proverb: "It is not wrong to go back for that which you have forgotten." In their own words, the Evangelical Covenant Church's Sankofa Journey is "an intentional, cross-racial learning journey that seeks to help Christians look back in order to move forward toward a righteous response to the social ills related to racism." This interactive experience visits historic sites of importance in the civil rights movement, places of oppression and inequality for people of color, while seeking to move participants toward healing the wounds and racial divides caused by hundreds of years of racial injustice in the United States.

I've done the journey several times myself, but the experience of my friend Austin Channing Brown really epitomizes the identification phase. One of the stops on the trip is a museum with a collection of graphic photographs documenting the horrific lynchings of black people in America. I'm sure you can imagine the impact. Looking at photo after photo after photo of young black men hanging from trees, or mothers hanging with their children, with white people often looking on in celebration, was intensely disturbing for the Sankofa group. Most of the group members couldn't speak. They got back on the bus in complete silence. There was a palpable tension. Finally the white members broke the silence. Understandably, they were eager to defend themselves and put some distance between themselves and the immense brutality of what they had just witnessed. *They* hadn't committed these terrible crimes, after all, and it was all such a long time ago.

Then a black student stood up, in obvious pain yet still calm, collected and quiet, and announced her conviction that *all* white people are evil. Shouting and disagreement erupted, and it was unclear how the group would be able to move forward from this experience.

Finally a white female student stood up to speak, and everyone seemed to hold their breath. But instead of another version of "please don't make me responsible for this," she said, "I don't know what to do with what I just saw. I can't fix your pain, and I can't take it away, but I *can* see it. And I will work the rest of my life to fight for you and for your children so they won't experience it." She started to weep, and her mascara streaked down her cheeks, leaving dark trails.

The bus was silent, and then my friend Austin said aloud, "She's crying black tears."

She was indeed crying black tears. The black students on that bus now felt that someone identified with their pain and the experience of their people, and it was a profound moment of identification for all of them. Instead of trying to dismiss it or explain it, the young white woman cried in empathy and solidarity with the black students in her group. *This* is what it means to see from the perspective of others.

Identification begins with an attempt to understand the other, and it delves ever deeper as participants take ownership of each other's stories. Identification is where former strangers begin to create a new community. It's where people create a *true* community through strategic storytelling, dialogue and active listening. It is in this phase that reconcilers learn that they must be open not just to thinking differently but also to relating differently with actual *people.* Instead of separating herself, the reconciler seeks to understand other people in her group and risks vulnerability. In the terminology of John Gottman, a psychologist known for his work on marital stability and relationship analysis, this is taking "bids."[4] It's putting out feelers to see if someone will take me in instead of rejecting me. It's reaching out and taking a risk to share our story with others.

THE POWER OF STORIES

One of the most helpful ways for members of a group to expand their understanding of who they are is to look at their stories and metaphors. We all live through metaphors. The stories that we tell ourselves *about* ourselves—those metaphors that we create in our own heads—suggest that we're okay. My mother used to always tell my siblings and me, "You can't be just *as good as*; you have to be *better than.*" That was her way of saying to her black children that the world is not necessarily fair and if we were going to succeed in life we would have to be better than our white counterparts. These stories we tell ourselves aren't always true, mind you, but they are comforting because they help us to make sense of our world. They give us security and identity, and they are what differentiates us from other people. In other words, *our* metaphors are different from *their* metaphors; *our* stories are different from *their* stories.

For all of us, personal change entails an alteration of those metaphors and the stories we've been telling ourselves. The leaders of your group can change the thinking of your group by changing metaphors and guiding the group into a new narrative. We learned back in the realization phase that the way we thought things are is not necessarily the way they really are. Now we must either shift our thinking or withdraw and back away from the process. We can shift into a preservation mode, or we can accept the challenge in front of us to be transformed by taking on new stories and metaphors. One way we can do this is by connecting our story to a bigger narrative with a more compelling mission.

BEING ON MISSION TOGETHER

When I was a campus staff member with InterVarsity Christian Fellowship in Southern California, I learned an important principle that has stayed with me ever since. It is simply this: fellowship springs from a shared mission. Contrary to popular belief, it's not the other way around. It's not enough to just be friends. It's not enough to hear someone's story and feel genuine compassion. While those things are certainly helpful, they are not enough to sustain a group over the long haul and bring about systemic change on a larger scale. Instead, we must focus first on a mission to which our group can be committed together.

Consider the military, or your favorite sports team. These groups are especially successful at building diverse communities because their members are on a mission together. Whether the goal is to defend the nation or win the Super Bowl, having a shared mission makes all the difference. If you are in the military, the men and women in your battalion might ordinarily be perfect strangers— possibly even enemies—but when you are in battle, all of that is forgotten. You are *one*. You are fighting and straining and praying for something together. So too with sports. Your teammate might be the *last* person on the planet you would normally associate with, but on the field, all that is forgotten as you log the hours and push yourselves to your physical limits in the shared dream of the ultimate crown. Fellowship, truly getting to know and bond with people in an intimate and life-giving way, comes from being on mission together.

A great example of what this looks like is demonstrated by a church-planting pastor and his young congregation on the South Side of Chicago.

As a white man establishing a multiethnic church in a predominantly black neighborhood, David Swanson knew that it was vitally important for him and his church to identify with their neighbors. To do this, they had to know and understand the concerns of the community and demonstrate that they were willing to help address these pressing issues. Although David is a deeply reflective person, he knows that he can't just sit quietly and listen all the time. Instead, he has to show members of the local community that he is on mission with them. He and his church have to empathize and demonstrate that they truly get their neighbors' needs for jobs, better education and protection from gun violence. They must therefore speak up and show up at rallies and community organizing events and participate in protests to draw attention to these pressing needs. Being trusted is one of the most vital factors for a multiethnic church in a monocultural context. So David and his church have worked hard to identify with their local community and build trust with their neighbors.

A turning point came one morning when David was conversing over breakfast with a leading black pastor in the community. The pastor said, "You will have trouble in this neighborhood because you are a white pastor."

David thought to himself, *Tell me something I don't already know!*

Then the black pastor quickly continued: "But don't worry about that, because I'll speak up for you." Basically this pastor was saying that he had observed integrity in David and his young church through their identification with the community, and he was willing to put his reputation on the line to vouch for their credibility.

When I asked David how this kind of trust and credibility had been built with that pastor, he told me that he partnered with him on a specific event. The black pastor had shared an idea he had to start a ministry called Prayer Around Schools. His vision was for every school to be adopted by a local church whose members would meet once a month and physically walk around the building, praying for the specific needs of the teachers, students, staff and administrators who attended and worked there. David volunteered his church, and they got involved in this effort. They identified a couple of schools near where they meet for Sunday worship services. For three years David and his multicultural church have prayed around two schools on the first Saturday of every month—in all types of weather! They pray for teachers in the church who teach at that school; they pray for the principals, with whom they have great relationships. They lift up specific prayer requests for the students and their parents, and they pray for financial resources and facility needs.

This is what that black pastor saw, and this is what it looks like when a group practices the identification phase of the Reconciliation Roadmap! It is a process of deconstructing our limited definitions of ourselves and reconstructing a new identity together, based on who God says we are—fearfully and wonderfully made, ambassadors of Christ, ministers of reconciliation and one new community through Jesus Christ. We begin to see ourselves and our cultural group not as the center of the human story, but as one essential part of God's story and the larger shared narrative of God's people.

⫸ GETTING PRACTICAL

Pray together.

- Ask God for racial and cultural wisdom and healing among those in your group.
- Pray that you will be able to communicate better with each other in order to deepen authentic intercultural relationships.

Explore your own identity.

- Name one family tradition (it may be associated with a holiday or annual event). How is it related to your ethnic heritage?

- Think about yourself in terms of some identifiable grouping, such as race, economic class, geographic origin, age group, gender or personal interests. What are some terms you use to describe yourself to others?

    1.

    2.

    3.

- Expand on these terms using stereotypes or negative connotations you've heard associated with them. (For example, "college-educated" might become "superior" or "snobby"; "middle-class" might be "average" or "run-of-the-mill.")

    1.

    2.

    3.

- How do you respond emotionally and intellectually to these stereotypes?

- What descriptive terms would you *like* to be used to characterize your particular ethnic heritage or family background?

- What aspects of your ethnic heritage have helped you to understand God? Reflect on this and give praise to God.

PLANNING FOR ACTION

The Preparation Phase

For it is not difference which immobilizes us, but silence.
And there are so many silences to be broken.

Audre Lorde

Each year I assign the book *Let Justice Roll Down* by John M. Perkins for my students at Seattle Pacific to read. One day while discussing the book, several of my students expressed concern about a very difficult experience Perkins recounted from his days working in Mendenhall, Mississippi. He was a Bible teacher and community leader there in the mid-1960s, and during those years he befriended a white man named Robert Odenwald. Odenwald was the pastor of the First Baptist Church of Mendenhall and was initially not at all interested in developing a friendship with Perkins, a black civil rights activist. Perkins persisted, though, and eventually these two men began spending time together, discussing their community and their mutual love of Scripture. Through this unlikely friendship, Reverend Odenwald began to see himself, his world, his community and his local church in new and challenging ways, despite the prevailing racial attitudes of his town and country.

During Odenwald's first in-depth encounter with Perkins, he discovered, much to his surprise, that the two men shared the same faith. When Perkins left that day, Odenwald was in tears. (I interpret that encounter as a catalytic event that propelled him forward into the realization phase.) Over the ensuing months, he and Perkins continued their conversations, and it appears that he moved along on the journey into the identification phase. He began to identify with Perkins as a brother in Christ who had the same hopes, dreams and beliefs as his own. Perkins's stories and experiences were becoming *his* stories and experiences. Through this new friendship, his worldview was changing, and he was eager to bring his church alongside him on the journey. As they continued their friendship, the two of them slowly and steadily worked to build a bridge between their two communities.

Now, before I go further to tell you about what was so troubling to my students, I must remind you that the Reconciliation Roadmap is applicable to both individuals *and* groups. Although this book is focused on building communities and organizations of reconciliation, the same process is a powerful transformation experience for an individual. Often many people in our groups refuse to take the reconciliation journey with us, so that we must go through the process by ourselves. Robert Odenwald gives us a glimpse of what it looks like for a person to move along the road alone. His church was not supportive of his shifting perspective on the established social attitudes of the town, and they resisted his encouragement to change. They did not appreciate his new sermons, and they ultimately rejected him, turning their backs on him. Over time, this severe rejection by his own community, and the inability to form a new connection with others in the fight for racial equality, overcame him. Sadly, John Perkins writes in his book, not long after their friendship had begun to flourish, Pastor Robert Odenwald committed suicide.

My students were devastated when they came upon this account, and wondered if Odenwald had been ill-prepared for the inevitable pushback he would receive. I don't know. This is an extreme example, but it is a sober reminder to all of us that we are about to cross a *significant* gulf when we enter the preparation phase. We are moving to the third landmark of the model, where things are no longer so straightforward. It's not just a matter of being able to count the number of diverse people who've joined our group or the innovative programs and activities that we can tick off. We are now in this fuzzy area that is nuanced to your specific situation and context. For many people the gulf is way too frightening, too wide and too daunting to navigate. This phase moves us from the personal and relational to the structural and the transformational, and the gap between the two is *huge*. This is where we make the decision to be in the game for real—now we're preparing to go public!

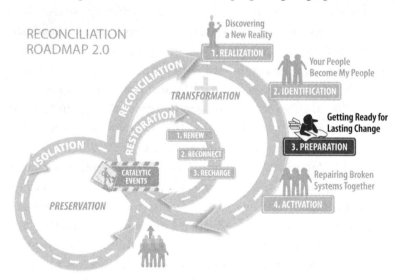

A CONSCIOUS CHOICE

As a consultant, I've been asked many times about when the reconciliation process tends to break down. Half-jokingly, I answer that

I usually get fired when people or groups enter into this, the preparation phase. Surprisingly, though, it is not because of a problem. Instead it's because people are doing well! The diversity crisis that caused the organization to reach out for help has been averted. They are now beginning to attract and build connections with more diverse people. They're thrilled that their group looks better, and people are pleased with the changes that they've made. They have invested a lot of time, money and attention in addressing the particular issues that caused people to feel unwelcomed or unsupported. As a result, they lose their sense of urgency, and they may well become satisfied and a bit complacent in their progress. Consequently, they quit prematurely and step off the road because they think they're already done! If a person or group is going to quit the journey, it happens in the preparation phase.

Folks typically tend to gravitate to the first half of the model, engaging in the realization and identification phases with urgency and focus. Once they have passed through those first two phases, people feel more adept at dealing with the issues of racial reconciliation. However, what they fail to realize is that *relational connections cannot be sustained without structural intentionality.* Structures to support our efforts toward long-term reconciliation have to be established, and it happens here, in the preparation phase.

This is hard work, and that's why the preparation phase is such a challenging stage—for organizations and individuals alike. It stretches us in painful ways and requires the development of "new wineskins." By this I mean that the old beliefs, patterns and practices that have worked in the past no longer fit with the new ideas and experiences that come with pursuing reconciliation and intercultural integrity. As Jesus says in Matthew 9, we cannot pour new wine into old wineskins, or they are liable to burst apart. Our old beliefs and our new beliefs cannot coexist. The way we operated in the past will not be sufficient to take us into the future. The new will demand that we do things differently. This is where many individuals and groups get stuck and even abandon the process altogether.

The preparation phase requires leaders and group members to make a conscious choice to count the cost of moving forward. What will be tossed out with those old wineskins? What do we stand to lose? What is this change going to cost us? In Robert Odenwald's story we see the most devastating response to those questions. He lost *everything*. The cost was that high for him, and he apparently felt unable to move forward on his own. Brian McLaren, the influential pastor and leader of the emerging church movement, once said that "the persecution that hurts the most isn't from 'the culture' but from one's own tribe."[1] This is what Pastor Odenwald experienced—rejection by his own tribe; and worse, he had nowhere else to go. He had not yet developed deep relationships and support networks with people outside his church community. I don't condone suicide, but I do understand the despair and fear that could cause a person like Pastor Odenwald to feel like he had nothing left.

That's why the preparation phase cannot be rushed or minimized. It is a challenging stage that should not be taken lightly. If we don't navigate this phase well, it could mean the death of all the good work that's been done thus far. We've worked hard over a significant period to build community through multiple trust-building efforts and interactions. If we're not careful with this next phase of structural change, we won't be able to retain the diverse people who are now a part of the beautiful, newly reconciled community that is forming.

SECOND-ORDER CHANGE

The work of the preparation phase begins with capacity building. This is where we determine what capabilities, resources, strengths, training and so on we need to help us move forward. This phase is about preparing for action that is not based in reaction. It is the beginning of what is called *second-order change*. This is significantly different from our usual attempts to bring about greater diversity by increasing the number of ethnically diverse members in our group. Numerical diversity is first-order change. It may resolve some aspects of the problem, but in the long run, unless second-order change takes root, the same cultural assumptions will operate within the group.

Second-order change is deciding to do things significantly or fundamentally different from how they have been done before. At this critical level, key assumptions about how things should work are addressed. It might mean the shifting of operational paradigms and result in structural changes being made within the organization. It might mean that the ways people interact, or believe they should interact, are renegotiated. It might mean new people being empowered to participate in innovative ways. It might mean that the leadership structures are reconsidered and the budget becomes a moral document that reflects our commitment to support reconciliation. This sort of structural change requires leaders and groups to create learning environments that incorporate transformation and change into their operating systems. If reconciliation and intercultural integrity are to be both achieved and sustained, then policies, procedures, structures and systems *must* go beyond adding numerical diversity. It's not just about the numbers.

FROM TRANSACTION TO TRANSFORMATION

This means that the participation of diverse group members in the development of an action plan is critical to the organization's transformation. If you want your group or your organization to change but you do not include diverse group members during the process, you aren't going to get very far! It is during the corporate decision-making process that groups ask questions of the organization like those posed by C. Otto Scharmer in his book *Theory U*:[2] What is my work? What is *our* work? What is underneath? What are we influencing? What is emerging? The answers to these questions have the potential to change the culture of your group. And it is what will ultimately begin the process of moving your group's commitment to reconciliation from private to public, beginning with a small group of leaders.

This is a major shift. There is a *big* difference between "transactional" and "transformational" change. For example, think of what you do when you go to a hotel to secure a room for the night. When you get to the hotel, you are not hoping for a life-changing experience. No! You just want a nice, clean room with a comfortable bed, for a reasonable price in a location that is welcoming and safe. If you agree to the rate and the terms of the agreement, you pay for the room and your transaction is complete.

On the Reconciliation Roadmap, such transactional changes take place in the first half of the model: things like recruiting more people from different backgrounds, hiring diverse staff members, translating information so as to provide bilingual reading materials, or increasing the number of women on your leadership team. Don't misunderstand. These are great transactions, and they give us a way to measure our progress. But the preparation phase is much more than that. It involves a transition from *transactions* to genuine *transformation*. Once you cross that line from transactional to transformational change, you begin to more fully understand that this is going to cost you something! It's what the preparation phase is all about—successfully making that transition from short-term connections to building a long-term community of reconciliation.

In short, the preparation phase prepares us for transformation. So, to return to our hotel analogy for a moment, if we had our eyes on transformation rather than a mere transaction, we would ask a different set of important questions. Now we are interested in the hotel's long-term success! We would want to know how the housekeeping staff is being trained and treated; we'd be concerned about opportunities for professional development and advancement; we'd pay attention to the reputation of the hotel and work to ensure that its business plan was viable in a competitive market. It's no longer only about completing short-term measurable transactions but about long-term sustainability and the ability to truly thrive.

ACCEPTING PARADOX

This movement from transactions to transformation reminds me of the biblical story of the rich young ruler in Mark 10:17-22. He was an earnest young man who had clearly done all the right things and wanted to do well in his life. Ultimately, though, when Jesus presented him with a chance for true transformation, he decided that the cost was just too high, and he chose to walk away. Here's what the Scripture text says:

> As [Jesus] was setting out on a journey, a man ran up and knelt before him, and asked him, "Good Teacher, what must I do to inherit eternal life?" Jesus said to him, "Why do you call me good? No one is good but God alone. You know the commandments: 'You shall not murder; You shall not commit adultery; You shall not steal; You shall not bear false witness; You shall not defraud; Honor your father and mother.'" He said to him, "Teacher, I have kept all these since my youth." Jesus, looking at him, loved him and said, "You lack one thing; go, sell what you own, and give the money to the poor, and you will have treasure in heaven; then come, follow me." When he heard this, he was shocked and went away grieving, for he had many possessions.

The preparation phase is similar. At this stage, many people decide that further pursuit of reconciliation costs too much, and they stagnate on their journey. Coaching folks through this stage into true transformation is no easy feat! It is so very challenging to discard patterns of thought and deed, especially when we believe they are necessary to sustain the life of our group and thus they have become second nature. It can be helpful in these murky places to remind ourselves of the centrality of reconciliation to the entire biblical narrative and our shared identity as humans in God's family. Then, in trusting relationships and with the effective leadership that has been established in the identification phase, groups can move more readily through preparation by developing clear benchmarks and measurable outcomes. In so doing, though, they will have to first grapple with paradox.

Earlier, in chapter 3, I discussed the powerful and unsettling role of chaos in catalytic events. Now once again we see change that comes through chaos in the preparation phase. Humans have a natural drive to preserve themselves, and chaos is typically avoided at all costs. Don't see this as negative. It's normal! The challenge comes in accepting that if there is any hope of birthing new life, chaos *must* be part of the environment for a time. For those who have been taught to think in a Newtonian or mechanistic way, the response to chaos is usually something along the lines of "Whoa, getting chaotic! We gotta calm this *down* and get things under control." Many of us see chaos as a death threat. It threatens the life of our group, so we must get things back under control. Instead, this phase asks us to see the paradox and learn to embrace the chaos as leaders without trying to control it. Easier said than done!

The most helpful way to manage our fear of extinction or fragmentation is through the clear sense of stability that a group can maintain if they know their core identity well. In other words, the organization has to keep adapting; but it keeps adapting in order to maintain its identity in different contexts and different experiences. According to author Margaret Wheatley in her book *Leadership and the New Science: Discovering Order in a Chaotic World*, organizations often veer off course when they lose their identity or primary reason to exist. So the most critical question that every company, church, organization or college must ask themselves is *Who are we?*[3] To know who you are and what your purpose is enables your group to maintain a sense of balance when you are in a state of disequilibrium.

Logically, then, this transition is very difficult for a person or group that is still in the process of figuring out their identity. It's like a church that has made a commitment to be multiethnic but has no clue what that really looks like. They have no role models to follow, and there is no church-growth conference for them to attend that will give them principles and strategies for success. This is the feeling of chaos that they must go through! We all crave stability and equilibrium. We crave strong structures to support us. But when we enter this transitional phase we must be willing to accept the paradoxical truth that we have to go through chaos to get to a more stable place. Basically, if we want stability we have to go through instability to get it!

MOVING FORWARD

Practically speaking, what does this look like? First it means that we have to enter into a time of prayer and discernment. It's imperative that we pause and ask God what we are uniquely called to do. In John 5:19 Jesus says, "Very truly, I tell you, the Son can do nothing on his own; but only what he sees the Father doing; for whatever the Father does, the Son does likewise." He said this in response to the religious leaders of his day who were angry that he healed a man on the sabbath who was sick for thirty-eight years. His answer to them suggests that before Jesus engaged in any form of ministry he understood that the Father God was already actively at work. Only then did he participate in what he saw the Father doing. This means that we can ask to see what God is doing in our neighborhood, our workplace, our church, school or city. Instead of feeling the need to respond to *every* need that presents itself, we can ask to be shown what the Holy Spirit is already doing in our context. Then we join and participate in *what God is already doing,* instead of creating the human agendas that so often lead to burnout and despair.

We do this because the work of reconciliation does not begin with us; it begins with God. Ultimately, I believe that reconciliation is a spiritual process. This might mean that you and members of your team take prayer walks around your community and ask the Holy Spirit to show you where God is already working. Don't rush the process. Don't proceed until you've gained clarity about what you are called to do. As you pray and discern, you may realize that you need a stronger biblical foundation to anchor your group in the work you hope to do.

Once, when working with a church whose pastor was deeply committed to diversity and reconciliation, we surveyed the congregation and asked members to name three Scriptures that supported their belief in multiethnic ministry. Most congregants could name only one, at most. The pastor was shocked! He had mistakenly believed that since he preached about reconciliation so often, the members of his church surely had the same scriptural convictions that he had. Instead, he learned that in order for his church to move forward they would first need to increase their biblical knowledge about God's heart for reconciliation and multiethnicity. So take your time and make sure your foundation is firm before moving forward.

Second, the leaders of your group need to strategize. Strategic planning is a crucial part of the preparation landmark. Ask yourselves, *What is our mission?* It's vital that the entire leadership core, and eventually the entire group, be able to clearly articulate and own your mission. Who are you? Where are you going? What's the plan for getting there? How will you know if you are being successful? The preparation phase is where goals are set and the leaders of the group can clarify the desired outcomes and the benchmarks that will indicate progress along the way. This is where policies, procedures and processes are developed to drive diversity and racial reconciliation change initiatives into the institutional culture. The leaders must provide coaching, tools, training, resources and technical assistance along the way as the group grows and stretches into this new understanding of who they are.

DARING TO GO PUBLIC

The preparation phase is also about facing our fears. This invitation into transformation can be scary! So start by asking yourself, *What am I afraid of?* You must be willing to know it and to name it. This is the only way you'll be able to do what is necessary to strengthen yourselves around it.

There are usually multiple levels to the things we fear. For example, if you are a black person in an organization where you constantly have to educate and be patient with others who seem insensitive to your concerns, you may wonder, *Do I have to be vulnerable* again *with no results?* If you are a white person who deeply cares about these issues, you might fear rejection or being misunderstood as you attempt to get involved. As a Latino person, you may fear that the real issues that impact your people will never get addressed. Native Americans may rightly fear that they will not be invited to the table and will be excluded from the process. And Asian American people, from so many different ethnicities, may fear being reduced to a monolithic group and not being understood for the rich diversity and complexity they bring to the conversation.

The preparation phase is where we face these very real concerns and prepare for sustainability over the long haul. We do this by naming the fear, assessing the risk and speaking the truth in love instead of letting our fears paralyze us. This is where we get ready to go public. It is the phase where we assess our capacity to publicly declare our intention to pursue reconciliation. We pray and discern what we are specifically called to do and what role we are specifically called to play. This is when your group prepares to be "built to last," to use the title of Jim Collins's book. It is the preparation for action that is not reactionary but well planned and thoroughly thought through. It is the beginning of structural change from the inside out that will change the way you operate. This is when you shift from merely additive notions of diversity. You no longer focus on adding more numerical diversity to your group or organization but focus instead on creating actual structures for diversity. At first, this may seem like a straightforward task, but it often requires waiting to determine exactly which kind of structures are really needed.

ACTIVE WAITING

River City Community Church, on the West Side of Chicago, gives us an example of what it looks like to go through the preparation phase. The church is in the Humboldt Park neighborhood, which is known for its dynamic social and ethnic demographic changes over the years. Since the 1970s, the Puerto Rican community has identified strongly with this area, but this is changing due to the influx of more African Americans and gentrification as upwardly mobile young white professionals move into the neighborhood.

Daniel Hill is the founding pastor of the church, and from the very beginning the vision and mission was for this congregation "to become a multiethnic community of Jesus followers that transform the city of Chicago through worship, reconciliation, and neighborhood development." For years Daniel and his leaders desired to develop a partnership with Casa Central, the largest Hispanic social service agency in the Midwest. It would be a huge blessing to partner with this organization that has been in existence since 1954, providing award-winning programming in response to the needs of the Hispanic community. However, Casa Central's staff have seen their share of eager young "do-gooders" come and go many times over, so for years they made Daniel and his church wait.

During that time the church included many young white professionals who felt like they knew better than the community what was really needed. They wanted the church to get more actively involved and to fix things faster. Daniel's hardest job in the preparation phase was holding back these action-oriented members and making them wait until they were invited to partner in community-led efforts. They had to learn how to measure action in terms of learning and investing in relationships, instead of solving problems and starting programs. They had to learn that the work of preparation is not passive at all! It's a different type of action. It's the hard work of being present and available, of listening and learning, of building trust and establishing credibility.

It took *five years* for the relationship between Casa Central and the church to change. That's a long time! But now the agency considers River City to be its primary church partner. It took those years of waiting until there was mutual buy-in and a long-term relationship built on trust.

This is no triumphalist story. Instead it's a picture of a church just patiently and actively waiting to be invited in. In the preparation phase we're not just twiddling our thumbs! We determine what types of structures and outcomes are really needed, and we clarify how to proceed.

As you can see from the experience of Daniel and his church, it's in the preparation phase that we are transformed into a new way of being. When we go through the transition into this phase, we really can't go back. The process is irreversible: once you begin, it is impossible to return to the exact way you were doing things before.[4] It's like going into a cocoon to experience the metamorphosis of a caterpillar into a butterfly. It will be frightening and uncomfortable. This work is very costly. But it is also immensely rewarding—and central to the gospel of Christ. I pray that you and your group or your church will have the courage to step forward into this phase, believing that the cost and the chaos of transformation are well worth it.

⫸ GETTING PRACTICAL

Count the cost.

> For which of you, intending to build a tower, does not first sit down and estimate the cost, to see whether he has enough to complete it? Otherwise, when he has laid a foundation and is not able to finish, all who see it will begin to ridicule him, saying, "This fellow began to build and was not able to finish." (Luke 14:28-30)

- What are some of the costs of pursuing racial and ethnic reconciliation for you and your group?

  1.

  2.

  3.

- What are some of the costs of *not* pursuing racial and ethnic reconciliation?

  1.

  2.

  3.

- What do you see God doing in your local context that might suggest where you and your group are being called to get involved?

7

DOING JUSTICE

The Activation Phase

> *Love is the only force capable of transforming an enemy into a friend.*
>
> **Martin Luther King Jr.**

> *Justice is what love looks like in public.*
>
> **Cornel West**

The *Year of Living Dangerously* is a drama about political strife in Indonesia in the 1960s. It follows a group of foreign correspondents in Jakarta on the eve of a coup to overthrow the president. A photojournalist named Billy Kwan is exposed to the highest strata of political society and the corruption that's a part of it. He's a highly intelligent and morally serious man of Chinese Australian descent who knows the truth. Throughout the film Billy is overwhelmed by a question that haunts him, which comes from Luke 3:10: "And the crowds asked him, 'What then should we do?'" This question becomes a haunting refrain throughout the movie until Billy finally decides to act. Although he is small in stature, he decides to risk his life by publicly expressing his outrage about the injustice suffered by the Indonesian people. He has come to the conclusion that it is morally wrong to be aware of injustice but stand idly by and not get involved. So he courageously hangs a sign outside a window of Hotel Indonesia along a military parade route, calling on the president to feed his people!

This story dramatically illustrates what the activation phase is all about—taking the risk to get actively involved. Here we determine how we can participate in efforts for justice and reconciliation. Here we join with others to cocreate solutions that can bring healing and wholeness to broken relationships and systems. Like a power cord that must be connected to an outlet in order to charge our technological devices, the reconciliation process cannot come alive until we plug into God's power and activate the insights we've acquired to become a vehicle for social change.

Reconciliation is not just for us. It is God's movement to transform the world so that all people on the earth can flourish. Reconciliation cannot be done in isolation. Instead, it must be done in solidarity with people whose concerns, problems and issues have become our own. It's at this landmark that we decide how to answer the challenging question *What then should we do?*

CARE

In order for individuals or groups to take action, they must find constructive ways to integrate their insights and the new skills they've gained with their everyday life. Therefore, the goal of this final stage is to "activate" the skills and competencies learned in the preparation phase by actively getting involved. The acronym CARE summarizes the basis of what must happen in this phase. It gives us a way to resist becoming paralyzed by the enormity of the problem or fear of our inadequacy: engaging in positive activity. In some ways, we don't know the reality of something until we begin to press into it. The preparation phase is essential, but the type of learning we receive in the activation phase is more from engagement and less from abstraction.

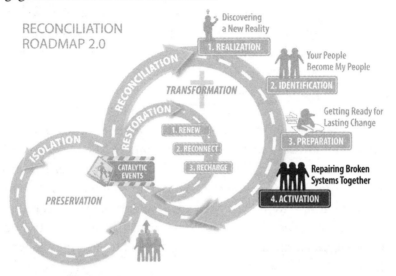

COMMUNICATE

The first step is to *communicate* what we have learned about a specific reconciliation or justice issue. Here it's important to clarify what I mean by a concern that is focused on justice. According to Eric Law, an Episcopal priest and international consultant on multicultural leadership, "Justice means equal distribution of power and privilege among all people."[1] Law explains that in order to do justice, it's essential for us to recognize that there is a difference between the ways that people from the dominant culture and others perceive power. He says, "The perception of personal power is our own understanding of our ability to change our environment."[2] In other words, some people are socialized to believe that they have power to change the status quo and make a difference in the world. However, those who perceive themselves as powerless will accept injustice as something they have to endure because that's "just the way it is." Understanding this discrepancy in the power differential is vital to fruitful caring. Law says, "When whites and people of color recognize that there are cultural differences in their perceptions of power, they take the first step toward doing justice."[3]

That's why it is so important for us to use our personal power to speak up and not keep silent when we see injustice happening in our workplace, our community, our campus and our place of worship. This is the hard work of sticking our necks out to speak truth to power. It is patriarchy, racism and socioeconomic discrimination that hinder people's ability to thrive as God intended.

There are several steps to this. First, we must develop a *communication strategy* that enables us to amplify the message and voices of others, especially those who are not being heard. Sometimes this will mean joining our voice with others in protest to focus public attention on a particular issue of injustice. Through peaceful public demonstrations like marches, sit-ins, boycotts and prayer vigils, we create a constructive tension that brings light to the urgency of the situation.

We also must learn when and how to tell our story and help others to tell theirs. Sometimes we need to do the talking. But many times we need to ensure instead that others are being heard. By "passing the mic" to underrepresented voices, we humanize the narrative, hearing, telling and interpreting their stories with integrity so that different communities can understand and learn from them. For some of us this might mean learning to speak another language that will allow us to be a bridge builder between communities and require us to interact with people on their terms. It also empowers people whose voices are not being heard to share their concerns in a language that fully expresses their heart. Through the process of learning to communicate between cultures, we develop compassion, empathy and humility as we submit to people with whom we might not normally interact.

Second, as we seek to communicate we can use our social media platforms to *raise greater awareness* about the problem. This can be uncomfortable for some folks! It is for me sometimes. But constructive tension can be powerful. Posting a status update or sharing an insightful link that unsettles people can be a good thing. I've learned the hard way that some people will become very upset when we connect reconciliation with politics and policies. As we communicate about these things, we will probably experience pushback and resistance from those who disagree. We might feel tempted to ease any and all tension—for ourselves and for others— but there is benefit to sitting in those tense spaces because it urges us forward to lasting change.

ADVOCATE

Then we must *advocate* for change. We must never think that we are finished once we have spoken up, be it on Facebook or in the boardroom. Talking isn't enough. We have to get moving! We need to expand the bandwidth of our conversations by influencing decisions within political, economic and social systems and institutions.

Once we establish principles that are rooted in our theology and our faith, we must vote and fight for political bills, corporate and institutional policies, neighborhood ethics and the like that reflect our faith-based principles. These should be very specific and concrete proposals that will make a difference in the lives of people *right now.*

An example of this for me is immigration reform. I was invited to speak at an immigration rally in Washington, DC, to help lobby members of Congress with other evangelical leaders. Our goal was to persuade our legislators to pass a bill that would improve our broken immigration system. While in DC, I heard stories about families being torn apart and children left alone because a parent was deported; undocumented women being raped or sold into slavery; undocumented men being robbed and physically assaulted without any possibility of legal or medical help. These stories forced me to realize that I cannot say that I love people if I don't care about the policies that negatively affect them. So when I took the podium to speak, I pledged my support and solidarity to be an advocate for immigration reform so that all people in the United States are given the dignity of having a fair path toward legal citizenship.

It won't look the same for every community. Different groups deal with different challenges. For some activation might mean looking into legal justice, immigration, sentencing disparities or racial profiling. For others it might mean championing justice around issues like unemployment, homelessness or predatory lending practices. Still others might closely examine housing discrimination, redlining, unequal access to education, environmental injustice, health care and government programs. Whatever it is, advocacy is a vital part of the activation phase and cannot be overlooked. As Rev. Vernon Johns, considered by some as the father of the civil rights movement, and predecessor of Martin Luther King Jr. as pastor of the Dexter Avenue Baptist Church, says, "If you see a good fight, get in it!"[4]

RELATE

We also need to *relate*. We have been transformed, and we need to be sure to surround ourselves, at least in part, with a like-minded community of people who will love us, forgive us and hold us accountable. Reconciliation is not something we can do alone. We need to be in a sustaining community that supports us and helps us to live out the values we espouse. This is easier said than done sometimes. It may take years before you find a community that will support your efforts and pursue justice alongside you.

In addition to being in community, relating involves building *partnerships*. Your group or church or organization will not work in a vacuum. You have to identify the social and structural issues that must be addressed in partnership with your local communities. Those committed to reconciliation must partner with indigenous, community-based leaders and learn from them. This will require asking questions about what the problems are and also being active participants in the community. Acts of justice must be contextually sensitive. Trust is built and credibility earned when people see that we are sincerely invested in the community and that we are affected by the same problems that concern them. Therefore, this relational focus will mean that an individual or organization must determine what community they feel called to relate to over an extended period.

This approach is very much aligned with the principles of John M. Perkins and the Christian Community Development Association (CCDA). One of the three principles that guide this movement of community renewal is "relocation." Those who desire to see change are challenged to move into the community and build genuine relationships with their neighbors. This means learning people's names, hugging their children, praying for their family when someone is sick, sharing a meal and mourning with them when a loved one dies. As we relate in this way, we foster reconciliation by embracing people, showing compassion and helping to address the issues of injustice that impact them.

EDUCATE

Lastly, we must *educate*. We can't rest on our laurels. We must commit ourselves to learning more about the ever-changing issues and our oft-precarious political landscape. We need to keep reading, keep asking questions and keep teaching what we know. We are influencing each other constantly, and when we CARE we take advantage of opportunities to build a larger movement for change.

On a more practical level, sometimes educating means that *we are teaching others how to activate*. Some people make it through the murky waters of the preparation phase only to arrive on the other side uncertain of the next steps. We have to encourage social engagement and lead the way. Others' lack of access to information and education limits their ability to fully participate in society. They are vulnerable to being taken advantage of by unscrupulous people and practices that perpetuate poverty and threaten our democratic process. As reconcilers we must use our influence to level the playing field for everyone by educating others about these real-life issues. The more we educate people, the more options they have for working collectively with us for social change. That's how education can become a very strong strategy to bring about justice and reconciliation.

ACTIVATING CARE

So what does it practically look like for us to live this out? A church in Englewood, New Jersey, shows us what it means to actively CARE. One Sunday, rather than having a regular worship service, Metro Community Church decided to walk around and pray for their community. They divided the city into areas within a four- to five-block radius around their church. The whole church went outside and prayed for homes, families, schools, businesses, offices, municipal buildings, streets and other churches. On that walk the pastor, Peter Ahn, prayed repeatedly and implored God to "break my heart for what breaks your heart." Eventually he had an idea: "We need to have folks in our church live among the neighbors in this community."

Englewood is a city located in New Jersey near the border of New York. With 27,533 people, it is the eighty-seventh most populated city in the state of New Jersey, with the largest racial and ethnic groups being blacks (34.1%), whites (27.4%) and Hispanics (22.2%). Like many cities, Englewood has its share of challenges. One pressing issue is that this city sends the highest number of juveniles to detention centers. Over time Peter and his church realized that the greatest need in their community was to help reach the "at-risk" youth in Englewood.

As a result of the prayer walk that Sunday, the church bought a house in the community. It's called the Metro House, and five single men live there, intentionally reaching out to serve their neighbors. One of the men is now running the program working with the most at-risk youth in the city. Metro LIFE (Living in Freedom Everyday) is an incredible holistic program that is both practical and intentional—including mentoring, life skills training, tutoring, working with families, college preparatory classes and justice advocacy. The Metro House has also become a safe haven for young people hoping to avoid gangs. Eventually the church hopes to build a community center that is a nonprofit organization in partnership with the city.

Government officials, school principals and the local police have taken notice. They are all impressed with this church's active involvement in its community. Off the record several of them have said to Peter, "These kids don't need another government program. They need Jesus!" This is the activation phase being lived out at its best—bringing healing, wholeness, justice and reconciliation to communities while pointing people to Jesus.

So you see that in the activation phase we roll up our sleeves and actively use the talents, abilities, resources and skills God has given us for reconciliation. We will make mistakes, and we will learn new things about ourselves and others as we go. This is how we CARE and prove our lives of intercultural integrity: not by being perfect or having all the answers but by taking the risk to get involved and try. Now it's time for you to go out there and put your CARE-ing into action!

⦀➤ GETTING PRACTICAL

Action planning: looking at knowledge, experience and relationships.

Knowledge. What more do you need to know? This could mean

- reading books on reconciliation
- attending additional or more in-depth workshops (possibly on related issues such as antiracism, gender, class or diversity)
- reading books by authors of races or cultures different from your own
- taking courses at a local university that address related issues
- paying attention to issues (news, politics, etc.) and concerns that are important in communities other than your own and

seeking to understand why there is a different perspective or worldview operating

Experience. What can you do, or what do you need to experience? This could mean

- attending a congregation whose members are primarily from a race and culture different from your own

- seeking to develop a partnership between your congregation and a congregation composed of a different race or culture

- spending a month or a year in a cultural or racial setting that differs from your own (immersion experience)

Relationships. How can you develop relationships consistent with your racial reconciliation values?

- Determine your circle of influence versus circle of concern.

  ▪ Use the two concentric circles below to help you prioritize your work. As you think about beginning the hard work of reconciliation within your particular group or context, what are you concerned about? List these concerns in the larger circle.

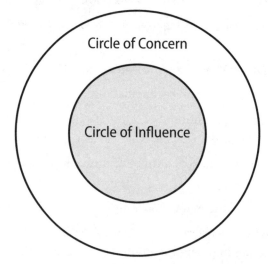

- Among these things, what are your areas of influence? That is, what do you have the power to actually do something about? It is important for individuals and the group as a whole to identify areas of concern and influence. Discussing this will help shape your strategic planning process as you begin to put these things into action.

- Strategic planning.

  - It is important to recognize that the implementation of these things will take several years. It doesn't happen overnight! As you strategically plan for the various areas of your group, be mindful of the stages and seasons of implementation:

    - immediate needs with clear action steps (1-2 years)

    - short-term strategies (3-5 years)

    - long-term strategies (more than 5 years)

  - As you prepare for this process, it's helpful for the group to answer the following questions as a team:

    - What existing structures, programs or practices are conducive to implementation of our reconciliation goals?

    - What are some other programs or structures that might be helpful to this initiative but do not yet exist?

    - What should we consider when setting our priorities?

    - How will the varying levels of priority and emphasis be managed and accounted for as we get further into the implementation? In other words, how can we be focused on the current strategy without losing sight of the initiatives set for the future?

    - What other questions or concerns do we have as we begin this process?

8

REPAIRING BROKEN
SYSTEMS TOGETHER

The Restoration Cycle

||||▶

I first met "Brother Reparations" when I was conducting a day-long reconciliation seminar at a church in Seattle, Washington. During my training, I interacted with the participants and had an open exchange that included questions and answers. This young black man raised his hand and asked why I didn't discuss reparations in my training on reconciliation. We talked about this for a few minutes, and eventually I gave him the microphone so everyone could hear what he was saying. Unbeknown to me, it deeply impressed him that I provided this opportunity for him to address the group. As a result, we developed a closer relationship and met several times afterward to discuss reconciliation and our views about social justice and the church. The issue of reparations was always a part of our conversations, and that's why I began to fondly refer to him as "Brother Reparations."

The following year, Bryan Stevenson, an American lawyer and social justice activist and the executive director of the Equal Justice Initiative, came to Seattle to speak at a special event about his groundbreaking book, *Just Mercy.* The event was sold out, but in one of our meetings Brother Reparations told me that he was a part of the sponsoring organization and could get me a ticket. So, on the night of the event, I went early and he got me a seat close to the front. To my surprise, I was sitting right next to a very close friend of mine!

At the end of Bryan Stevenson's presentation, he opened a time for questions and answers. The very first hand that went up was Brother Reparations. I nudged my friend and said to her, "I don't know what he's gonna ask, but it's gonna have something to do with reparations!" Sure enough, when Bryan Stevenson called on him, he asked in a loud voice, "Mr. Stevenson, do you believe in reparations?"

Bryan Stevenson gave an answer that I will never forget. He said, "Of course I do! But anybody can write a check. Real reparations would be to fix what was actually broken. For example, black people in this country were denied the right to vote. White people brutalized, terrorized and killed black people for trying to vote for over a century. So, to repair that, white Americans would automatically give all African Americans the right to vote on their eighteenth birthday! In fact," he said, "if you're an elderly African American, we would pick you up and drive you to the polls to vote! Now *that* would actually repair what was really broken!"

That comment had me reeling as I left the event that night. While I was driving home, a Scripture came to mind that I hadn't thought about in years. It was Isaiah 58:12, which says, "Your ancient ruins shall be rebuilt; you shall raise up the foundations of many generations; you shall be called the repairer of the breach, the restorer of streets to live in." Then I heard this phrase well up in my soul: "repairing broken systems together." That night I knew I would update my message and model to include reparations more clearly with this new understanding and awareness of what reconciliation really entails.

THE WORK OF REPAIR

Over the course of my work as a speaker and reconciliation leader, the question I'm asked most frequently is, *How?* People from all walks of life, from all types of churches, institutions and schools come up to me and say, "But . . . how? How do we actually do it? What does it really mean to reconcile? What does it mean to be a Christian activist for reconciliation?"

My answer has continued to evolve and sharpen over time. After my epiphany on my drive home from the Bryan Stevenson event, I've come to firmly believe that to actively participate in the work of reconciliation means to repair broken systems together. Real reconciliation is more than relational togetherness between people from diverse racial, ethnic and cultural backgrounds. This limited perspective has caused the concept of reconciliation to grow stale for many people. They are tired of the relational approach that Christians have used repeatedly because it does not lead to any real change in the systemic inequities that persist in our society today.

Real reconciliation repairs the inequity in systems and structures that are deeply rooted in the historical realities that produced the divisive relationships that are still operative in our racialized society. That's why we must take seriously the need to repair the actual harm that's been done in creating the social injustices taking place in our world today.

This is where the concept of reparations intersects with the work of reconciliation. This word may have frightening connotations for some people, but I believe that a closer and more objective look at it will help us to appreciate its true meaning. I have come to believe that *reparations* means seeing what is actually broken and repairing *that*. This is the work of God, is it not? And we are called to join in this reconciling work of God. *This* is what it looks like to reconcile. It is to be the "repairers of the breach and the restorers of streets to live in," just like the prophet Isaiah calls us to be as God's people.

This clearer understanding led me to update the activation phase of my Reconciliation Roadmap model to identify where the work of repairing broken systems specifically takes place in the reconciliation cycle. The updated components are highlighted in the diagram.

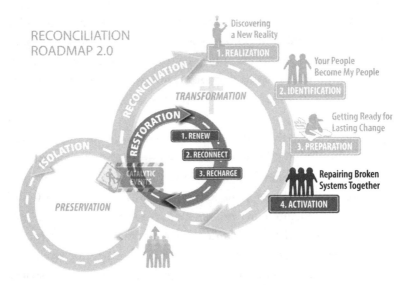

THE IMPORTANCE OF RESTORATION

In addition to updating the activation phase, you will also notice that I have included the restoration cycle as a new aspect of the reconciliation process. As my understanding and application of this work have evolved, the Roadmap 2.0 model now reflects the need for people of color to have opportunities for restoration as a part of their reconciliation journey.

This cycle is distinctly different from the isolation cycle, where people pull out or refuse to participate in the reconciliation process. Instead, the restoration cycle acknowledges that people of color are constantly doing the work of reconciliation and embodying the tension of living and working in a racialized society. Therefore, it is vitally important to affirm intentional time for them to take breaks from engaging in mixed-race and dominant-culture settings and have space to renew, recharge and reconnect. This ability to restore strengthens one's resolve to continue on the reconciliation journey and is identified by the following aspects.

1. Renew. It is vital to provide institutional support that enables those who are weary from the ongoing battle of working for reconciliation to rest and have chances for self-care, solitude, prayer and lament. This allows them to be replenished, refilled and made whole again. This may also include creating gathering spaces for people of color to meet regularly with each other or providing resources for an ethnic-specific retreat for the purpose of being refreshed.

2. *Recharge.* The physical and emotional toll of living and working in a racialized society is debilitating and exhausting for people of color. Therefore, we need the intentional creation of life-giving environments that address these needs by providing opportunities to be strengthened, nurtured and replenished. An example of this might be hosting a sacred time of lament in your ministry after a racial tragedy, inviting people to gather and hold each other in prayer.

3. *Reconnect.* For people of color in dominant-culture ministries, it is necessary to affirm the need to connect with others from their ethnic and cultural backgrounds. This provides a safe space to be understood and to reconnect with God and others in culturally familiar ways. This ability to step away from the battle enables people of color to refocus their thoughts and recommit to their purpose and desire to engage in reconciliation. To help facilitate such gatherings, a ministry or organization may want to dedicate a specific space where people of color have artifacts, music and other resources that are culturally relevant and affirming.

Additionally, part of the impact of a racialized society on African Americans in the United States has been the deconstruction of their historical narrative and identity. For ministries on this reconciliation journey, sponsoring DNA testing can serve as a means for African American members to reconnect to their heritage and reaffirm their origins in a life-giving way. What a gift it would be for the church to support African Americans in the process of restoring and reclaiming their narrative and identity as a part of the reconciliation journey. This would be an act of helping to repair what has actually been broken!

At this point, one may wonder whether the restoration cycle can also be a place of refuge for white leaders. For the most part, the answer is no. I recognize that there is a negative impact on everyone living in a racialized society, but the toll on people of color and on those who are white is very different. For whites, it's impossible to fully internalize the concept of "whiteness" as being good. The problematic nature of whiteness produces guilt and shame that paralyzes, causing denial, silence and inactivity. This then limits their ability to engage in the work of reconciliation and racial justice. Therefore, it is necessary to take the implications of whiteness more seriously in order to help whites break free from the distorted sense of identity they have internalized from the narrative of racial difference.

However, there are white allies who have been fighting on the front lines for years against racist and unjust systems. These people are actively working to repair broken systems with people of color with whom they are in community and solidarity. In this case, their community will care for them by inviting them into the restoration cycle so they can avoid burnout and have a chance to rest and be renewed. For others who are white and newer to the work, they should consider meeting regularly with other white reconcilers to connect, share resources, learn together and support one another's continued growth and awareness so that they can be better advocates for their sisters and brothers of color.

GETTING PRACTICAL

As Christian believers, we must be actively looking for broken systems and then setting about the difficult work of repairing them. We are called to repair these broken systems *together*. That means we work in humble partnership with those who are being negatively affected by those systems. We don't come in from the outside calling the shots or telling people in their community what we think is best for them. Instead, we humbly live and learn among people who slowly affirm our credibility and educate us about the complex realities they face and what, therefore, must be done.

As we build these mutually beneficial, life-changing, community partnerships, we will come to see that there are many broken systems all around us. Think of it: in the United States alone, our broken systems include but are certainly not limited to voting, incarceration, housing, education, economic injustice, immigration, health care, environmental exploitation, gender inequity, sexual harassment, lack of accessibility for those with disabilities, abuse of children and the elderly—and the list just goes on and on. This is why we must have an approach to reconciliation that is focused on repair and not concerned only with promoting crosscultural and relational tolerance and appreciation. However, I agree with author Jennifer Harvey, who writes in her book *Dear White Christians: For Those Still Longing for Racial Reconciliation* that this work of reconciliation focused on reparations will not be easy. She says,

> Repair offers no easy answers, nor any final solutions. . . . But repair does generate a clear, compelling standard by which to organize our activism and move from an unflinching honest look at the differential impact of white supremacy into actions that attempt to address and redress that impact.[1]

Ultimately, our activation of reconciliation is an effort to make things right. We are called to join God in the work of making things right. With this goal in mind, there are so many ways that Christ-followers can fight for justice and rightness. There are so many ways, every day, for every person to work on making things right in the world. So start looking. Start looking for what God is doing in your city and in your local context. Start looking and then join with those actively working to repair broken systems around you. Here are some examples of what *reconciliation for real* looks like.

As a young lawyer hot out of law school Bryan Stevenson found himself in Atlanta, Georgia, working for the Southern Center for

Human Rights. While he was there, he discovered vast disparities and bias against the poor and minorities in our nation's criminal justice system. I'm certain Stevenson wondered what difference he could possibly make. What could one man do against the system? But he has since devoted his life to challenging the system every chance he gets. He founded the Equal Justice Initiative and has assisted in securing relief for dozens of condemned prisoners, advocated for poor people and developed community-based reform litigation aimed at improving the administration of criminal justice. That's #Reconciliation4Real.

A man at my church in Seattle takes fellow Christians to the local mosque on Friday nights in an effort to break down barriers between Christians and Muslims. That's #Reconciliation4Real.

One of my son's best friends, Bethany, stuck her neck out on Facebook and posted a letter to the black community after the AME shooting in Charleston, South Carolina. That's #Reconciliation4Real.

Each year my entire congregation writes letters to Congress as part of Bread for the World's letter writing campaign to fight world hunger at the policy level. That's #Reconciliation4Real.

One of my fellow pastors and his wife gave up a year's wages to start a nonprofit in an effort to alleviate extreme global poverty. That's #Reconciliation4Real.

Churches that open their doors as safe havens for refugees are practicing #Reconciliation4Real.

Schools and universities that provide safe spaces for their LGBTQ students are practicing #Reconciliation4Real.

Families who uproot themselves and put jobs and school on hold in order to spend several months in Chios, Greece, assisting refugees coming in on crowded boats are practicing #Reconciliation4Real.

Learning your students' names and making sure you are pronouncing them properly is #Reconciliation4Real.

Celebrating the work and the art and the efforts of people of color, that's #Reconciliation4Real.

Telling stories that might not otherwise be told, that's #Reconciliation4Real.

Organizing other students at your school to advocate diversity on campus, that's #Reconciliation4Real.

When young people are protesting and a church provides comfort, care, medical support and places of safety and rest, that's #Reconciliation4Real.

Educating yourself so that you can cast your vote for politicians whose policies aim to repair broken systems rather than perpetuating oppression and white supremacy, that's #Reconciliation4Real.

Recognizing the reality of the posttraumatic stress that can come from living in a racialized society, from having to witness the death and destruction of your people on a daily basis, that's #Reconciliation4Real.

Understanding and speaking up about environmental injustices like the use and exportation of toxic pesticides, that's #Reconciliation4Real.

Advocating for better mental health care, that's #Reconciliation4Real.

All of these are tangible examples of actions that anyone can do, steps that anyone can take in order to restore broken relationships and systems to reflect God's original intention for all creation to flourish.

9

STAYING THE COURSE

Living Out Holistic Transformation

There is a need for . . . materials of refreshment, challenge and renewal for those who [are] intent upon establishing islands of fellowship in a sea of racial, religious, and national tensions.

Howard Thurman

How will you know when you've been successful?"

This was a question I was asked by Cecil Crawford, an early financier of Ticketmaster who established the Maggie Sloan Crawford award at Olivet Nazarene College in honor of his mother. I was completely caught off guard by his question, and after a few minutes of fumbling for a good answer, I said something that wasn't very clear or convincing. I was really embarrassed! Years later I still felt frustrated with myself for not having a better answer to such an important question.

But I am finally ready to give him an answer. I now understand that Mr. Crawford was asking the question from a business perspective. In his world, success is measured by tangible and quantifiable results. However, from a Christian vantage point, spiritual and moral values guide our intended outcomes, and they are not easily measured by those same metrics. Reconciliation is truly a journey, not a destination. It is a process that leads to personal, spiritual, social and systemic transformation. It's a mystery—a discovery process that does not take us back to where we were before but invites us into a story that is bigger than our own. *That's* how I would answer the question now, and that is exactly what your journey will look like as well: you will know you are on a true reconciliation journey if it is messy and complicated and beautiful and transformational.

Reconciliation is a dynamic process *and* an objective. Like all living systems, reconciliation is a nonlinear process that is progressive and at times cyclical in nature. Having gone through the process once doesn't mean that you have "arrived." Further growth and transformation are continually before you, and you may find yourself perpetually on the journey.

Maybe you walked through the various phases when you were younger, but now, years later, you find yourself in the midst of another catalytic event and discover your worldview shifting yet again. Maybe you've been vocal and active on issues of immigration, and now you find yourself working with urban youth and fumbling your way through the phases afresh. Whatever it is, you can count on this being an ongoing process and lifelong journey.

So what keeps us on the road to reconciliation? When things get messy and uncomfortable, what motivates us to keep pressing into those hard spaces? If we don't have metrics and checklists with tangible outcomes, how do we endure for the long haul? We need to understand the dynamics of the journey and to focus on a few key skills that will help us stay the course and resist derailment.

UNDERSTANDING THE PROCESS

All natural living systems go through cycles. This important truth is described in the S-Curve model, a theory used to help monitor the growth or progress of a particular project. I was introduced to this theory while in Belize, in the rainforest about twelve miles south of the capital city, Belmopan. I was there to learn about an organization called PathLight, which focuses on educating young people with the hope of transforming the country by breaking the cycle of poverty and offering hope through faith and learning.[1] During that visit I met a woman who is an organizational consultant, and she helped me understand the S-Curve as a model for organizational change.

The bottom of the S-curve illustrates the beginning of the process, which is full of experimentation and new growth. This is where innovative ideas are born and things are not very systematized. It's like the beginning of a new church plant or a start-up company. It's pretty chaotic, but the people involved are all in. There's passion and a sense of mission. Everybody's energized. All hands on deck! I remember hearing the pastor of a very large church outside Chicago recount stories about the early days of how this prominent congregation got started. Its first worship space was a movie theater. Every Sunday they had to sweep up all the popcorn and trash (and sometimes even vomit!) that moviegoers had left the night before. For two years the pastor and his friends pitched in and helped do anything and everything that was needed for this fledgling new church to survive. Eventually the church outgrew its space at the theater and purchased a plot of land that is still its home today.

Then there comes a time when it is necessary to systematize in order to sustain growth. Structures and systems are put in place, which enables intense growth to happen. This is illustrated by the straight line that emerges from the curve at the bottom of the model.

After some time, the group or organization reaches a point of stagnation or "stabilizing." This is called the "bifurcation point." This is the place where it is clear that if it keeps going in the same direction, it will eventually languish and commence the slow process of decline. People can show up, sing the same songs, do the same jobs, but the life and energy are gone. At the bifurcation point, leaders have to recognize and name this stagnation. They must step back into the place of innovation and chaos because they realize that the current systems are no longer working. The way out of this stagnation is to ask new questions.

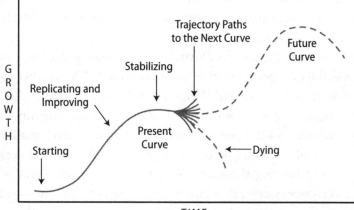

In natural living systems, anomalies come from the outside. Therefore, when stagnation occurs, a seeker of reconciliation must ask, What are the outside pressures? What are the anomalies that are forcing us to recognize that we need to lower productivity for the long-term health and growth of the organization?

At the basis of growth for living systems, the questions are really most important. There is always a need for questions, because the pressures from the outside are constantly demanding something new of us—a new approach, new people, a new perspective, new questions. Answers are usually temporary. Finding answers may be satisfying in the short run, but to move along to the next curve, we must get back to asking the deeper questions. This is what will re-energize and refuel us to keep moving deeper into the reconciliation process.

A group of evangelical leaders and I experienced this when we went to Ferguson, Missouri, to participate in a faith roundtable concerning the social unrest and civil rights movement that was emerging across the United States. While there, we met with a group of young leaders who had been protesting against police injustice for 117 days straight! Many of them had left jobs and college to put their lives on the line for the movement. After our meeting with them, these young leaders sent us the following text message:

> We are coming up on the annual Jewish holiday of Chanukah. You all know the story: the Jewish people were downtrodden and oppressed. They rose up in rebellion and fulfilled their duty to win. But when the Jewish leaders retook the Temple, they had another crisis. The Eternal Flame, symbol of the continuing presence of the divine, had only oil enough for one day. They sent runners to get more oil, but it took them eight days to return with the needed fuel. Miracle of miracles, the one day of oil lasted for eight days!
>
> We are our burning flames in this moment. On August 9 we hit the streets with no assurance that we could sustain ourselves for more than a few days. Yet our flame has now burned for 117 days! This is a miracle for which we need to rejoice.
>
> Yet remember, the Jewish people did not sit back and rely solely on God's miracle. They got busy and ran to supply the physical fuel that was needed. God's miracles do not relieve us of our duty to support the cause of justice.
>
> As you go home to your communities, please take this message with you. You are the ones we are sending out for more fuel. It is a sacred mission.

These young people exerted "outside pressure" to force us to ask ourselves new questions about our readiness to really get involved. It was a willingness to ask and be asked challenging questions that gave birth to the Jesus Movement in the 1960s, the "seeker-sensitive movement" in the 1980s and the emergent church movement in recent history. For many believers, each of these was a fresh, new, creative way of reimagining what it meant to be the church. New multiethnic church plants grew out of them; artists and creative people were invited to bring their gifts and participate in exciting ways; innovative incarnational evangelism strategies emerged; and people who were disenchanted with the church came back and experienced Jesus for the first time.

What are the questions that are fueling your church, organization or academic institution? What questions are your systems consciously or unconsciously asking? These adaptive, life-giving questions are the drivers for all living things.

KEY SKILLS TO HELP US STAY THE COURSE

In many endeavors, there are fundamental skills that must be learned if we want to be successful. In my experience, there are eight basic skills that are essential for those walking along the path of reconciliation:

- information gathering
- reflective thinking
- strategic storytelling
- community building
- intercultural communication
- inductive learning skills
- conflict resolution
- problem solving

First we must learn the skill of *information gathering*, which enables us to identify the real or underlying issues, understand the complexity of the problem and make an informed decision about how to respond. This requires the ability to collect information from various sources so that we are exposed to different perspectives.

Next we have to think critically about this information, assimilate it and relate it to other aspects of our experience to determine if it is true. This skill is called *reflective thinking*, and it requires a level of social maturity that enables a person to distance themselves from a group or peer pressure, take different perspectives, make independent judgments and take responsibility for their own actions.

Then, as we learn more about others, it is important to know how to *tell our story in a strategic way* so that we can engage with others, build trust and connection, offer our story and receive theirs. For this we need to be able to answer questions like the following:

- What are the key components of my story?
- How have I/we been shaped by our pursuit of reconciliation?
- What story do I/we want to be known for?

This skill might also be used to include ethnic diversity in the vision or mission statement of an organization. It helps to clarify and declare what narrative the group is intentionally planning to work toward. Then, based on this vision, leaders can determine how to measure the progress of their staff and departments in exemplifying this corporate story.

Sharing stories is a central skill in *community building* and fostering *intercultural communication*. When people from different cultures exchange information, there are many unspoken attitudes, beliefs and norms that can impact their ability to communicate effectively. The ability to self-disclose and listen empathically is an essential aspect of strategic storytelling and is also the core skill of intercultural communication. Therefore, leaders need to provide experiential learning opportunities for all staff or members to increase their communication skills. This is especially true in situations when the stakes are high, when there are strong emotions and opposing opinions. In these challenging circumstances, sharing one's own story can be a way to move beyond the impasse that arises when "facts" are being debated; storytelling allows people to connect beyond the words being spoken. This is vital to community building and learning how to work together toward reconciliation.

Another skill that is essential in building a reconciled community is the *ability to engage in inductive learning*. This is the process of uncovering meaning through observation, interpretation and application as we interact with new information and circumstances. As we observe, ask questions and struggle with others in community to understand what things really mean, we begin to discover truth for ourselves. This can apply to studying Scripture together or to gaining clarity in new situations.

As we do this, it's normal for there to be conflict along the way. In fact, conflict should be expected! When a community is made up of individuals from different religious, social, ethnic and educational backgrounds, we are bound to step on one another's toes. Therefore, *conflict resolution* and *problem-solving* skills are critical if there is any hope for reconciliation to actually take place. This means that we must each be aware of our own conflict style and how we cope under stress. It also means developing a problem-solving strategy, such as naming the problem, developing alternative solutions, monitoring progress, managing stress and encouraging adaptive decision making. Further, we may need to ask for outside accountability to help us navigate the inevitable challenges. It can also be helpful to invite outside analysis to objectively evaluate our ongoing commitment to diversity and reconciliation.

THE POWER TO PRESS ON

Individuals and groups continually cycle through the phases of reconciliation. I believe that in addition to our human efforts and intentions, the process contains an element of mystery. It takes significant energy to begin and sustain ourselves and the groups we lead in the reconciliation process. Catalytic events provide opportunities to reengage and also serve as benchmarks in the history of our various groups. However, becoming people who genuinely embody reconciliation day in and day out is difficult. There are times when we grow weary in the struggle and our energy to keep moving forward all but disappears. In those times we need the power and the hope that only God can give. God intervenes in the process to bestow us with the strength we need to stay the course. The Holy Spirit guides us, nourishes us and pushes us forward.

We must also *trust the process*. This journey will change us. That much I know for sure! I have observed over the years that people often fail to give enough credit to the transforming power of the process itself. We want to wait to give ourselves credit only after we feel like we have arrived or achieved our goal. If you are reading this book, you are already in the thick of the process, and that is transformative! Reconciliation is less about the destination and more about the journey.

Therefore it's important that we *build monuments*. We need to mark what we have done and the small accomplishments we've made along the way. This is how we increase our patience and that of our fellow travelers. We can so easily become disillusioned and discouraged if the process doesn't happen quickly, so these reminders of what God has done and the victories we have won will lend us encouragement and strength on the road to reconciliation.

Not sure how to build a monument? Maybe the mission statement of your church or organization has been changed to reflect a clear commitment to the value of diversity. Mark that moment! Make it something to celebrate and remember every year. Have a graphic designer create a plaque of your mission statement that can be prominently displayed for all to see. Or maybe you can name and acknowledge the key people who came or assumed strategic positions of leadership to spearhead your new initiative and move it forward. If you received significant financial resources or sacrificial giving that demonstrated God's faithfulness to provide for reconciliation and make it a reality, find a way to honor it. Have artists paint a beautiful vision of diversity that folks can see every time they walk through the doors. Or plant a tree outside your building.

One of my students was an art major and reconciliation studies minor at Seattle Pacific University. She created a beautiful sculpture of Jacob's well, where Jesus met the Samaritan woman in John 4. It became a powerful symbol of reconciliation for all of us on campus.

Another example was when we experienced a significant answer to prayer at the church I attend. A missionary was released from prison in North Korea after years of captivity with no diplomatic solution in sight. When we learned that he had been set free, oh, how we rejoiced! We have found ways to mark that moment so that we can remind ourselves when we face discouragement in the future.

Build monuments to mark and commemorate the significant moments in the history of your group or organization for folks to rally around and use to renew their strength when fatigue creeps in.

The Roadmap itself can serve as a monument. Yes, reconciliation is an ongoing process, but we are not running in place! We *are* making progress. The Roadmap reminds us about the power of the phases that lead us to transformation. Personal, spiritual and social transformation happens when we engage meaningfully with diversity. We will all continue to have biases, stereotypes and prejudices. These things die hard and will continue to rear their ugly heads for as long as we live. But we challenge those assumptions every time we hear and obey that still, small voice inside our heart calling us to

- go into someone's home and have personal contact with them
- sit at a table in the cafeteria with a different group of kids and get to know them
- get involved in an organization to improve the community or address a pressing problem

Our interaction with difference can lead to transformation, so we must look for and welcome the opportunities God brings us to do so. *This* is the dynamic energy that gives us strength to stay the course and inspires us to keep moving toward the vision of true reconciliation.

ⅢⅢ➤ GETTING PRACTICAL

Evaluate: The Five-fold Test
Gary Walters, president of the Evangelical Covenant Church, developed a tool of evaluation called the Five-fold Test.[2] This evaluation tool measures growth or change related to ethnic diversity in various areas of a group or organization. The following outline is based on his test. Discuss these questions as a group.

- Has growth happened in the following five areas?

  - *Population:* What is the racial and ethnic makeup of people on all levels of our organization or group?

  - *Participation:* Who is involved in the organization? Does the participation reflect the population?

  - *Power:* Who holds the power in our group/organization? Who makes decisions? Who influences the population? Who is leading this organization? Who initiates changes in direction?

  - *Pacesetting:* Who takes risks and is asking new questions on behalf of the group/organization? What new, innovative strategies, ideas or approaches to multiethnic ministry are coming out of your group?

  - *Purposeful narrative:* How has your group/organization's story changed as a result of your reconciliation journey? Who is telling this new story in a purposeful way? What voices are involved in the narrative?

- Consider these "Eight Habits of Interculturally Competent Leaders." How does your leadership measure up?

  - Include ethnic diversity in the mission/vision statement of the organization.

  - Measure the progress of all staff regarding their growth in ethnic diversity—"we measure what we value and we value what we measure."

  - Include intercultural competence in the training process for all new staff.

  - Identify and use existing strengths and capacities in the organization to increase the intercultural competency of all members.

  - Coordinate all of the multicultural and ethnic diversity–related initiatives (activities, programs, events, policies, etc.) in the organization.

  - Provide experiential learning opportunities for all staff to increase their awareness and expose them to exemplary ethnic diversity models.

  - Provide tools and ongoing training for all staff and leaders to develop their intercultural competency skills.

  - Invite outside accountability to evaluate the organization's sustained commitment to racial and ethnic diversity.

Conclusion

A VISION OF A
FLOURISHING FUTURE

This may only be a dream of mine, but I think it can be made real.

Ella Baker

Every three years, a very large student missions conference called Urbana is held in the United States. Thousands of delegates gather from around the world during the days between Christmas and New Year's to discern and wrestle with fundamental questions about God, themselves and where they're going. I have been blessed to speak at this great event, and I can attest that it is a life-changing experience for many people. For me, Urbana is one of those rare opportunities to participate in a multinational, multi-ethnic, multilingual global event that provides a taste of "heaven on earth." What people encounter at Urbana gives them a model for what can be replicated in their own contexts around the world. It's transformational! And it's a small example of what is possible on the road to reconciliation.

THE BELOVED COMMUNITY

Most of us think we know what *shalom* means. We think it means "peace" or "tranquility." But the word is actually much more profound than that. *Shalom* is the Hebrew word that encapsulates the Hebrew understanding of *the world as God intended it to be*. It's the word most often used in Scripture to describe God's intentions for the world.

In his book *The Wolf Shall Dwell with the Lamb*, Eric Law refers to shalom as the "peaceable realm" described in Isaiah 11:6-9:

> The wolf shall live with the lamb,
>   the leopard shall lie down with the kid,
> the calf and the lion and the fatling together,
>   and a little child shall lead them.
> The cow and the bear shall graze,
>   their young shall lie down together;
>   and the lion shall eat straw like the ox.
> The nursing child shall play over the hole of the asp,
>   and the weaned child shall put its hand on the adder's den.
> They will not hurt or destroy
>   on all my holy mountain;
> for the earth will be full of the knowledge of the LORD
>   as the waters cover the sea.

This is a vision of all creation living together in harmony and peace. There is no fear of being destroyed by the other. Instead, Law explains that this place of shalom is characterized by love, equality and justice. "Our vision of the Peaceable Realm is not based on fear. Instead, it is based on the lack of fear. . . . This lack of fear is created by the even distribution of power. . . . To do justice, then, is to be able to see and recognize the uneven distribution of power and to take steps to change the system so that we can redistribute power equally."[1] In this new realm, it is our righteous God who causes us to balance the scales and ensure that power is shared equally.

Not only that, but God's shalom also means the end of violence and war. In Isaiah 2:4 the prophet says,

He shall judge between the nations,
    and shall arbitrate for many peoples;
they shall beat their swords into plowshares,
    and their spears into pruning hooks;
nation shall not lift up sword against nation,
    neither shall they learn war any more.

Instead of developing weapons of destruction, people will create tools that benefit humankind. Enemies will make peace, and there will be no more violence. The whole creation, including the environment, will flourish. There will be no more poverty, pain, sickness or disease. No more crying. No more dying. No more injustice. No more lying. No more inequality. No more sexism. No more discrimination.

The book of Revelation also gives us a glimpse of shalom. It's a sneak peek. It shows us what it will look like when the kingdom of God comes in full. It shows us the world as God intended it to be. Specifically, Revelation 7:9 paints a vivid picture and tells us what to expect when the kingdom of God comes: "After this I looked, and there was a great multitude that no one could count, from every nation, from all tribes and peoples and languages, standing before the throne and before the Lamb." In this vision the kingdom of God includes men, women and children of all ages from every race, every tribe, every nation and every language. Those particular parts of our personhood aren't going to be erased. No! We're going to keep our skin color. We're going to keep our language, our lingo and our culture. The world as God intended it is a multicultural, multilingual, multiethnic and multinational place!

Can you imagine? Think about it for a moment. What will it look like? What will it smell like? Sound like? When I imagine it, I can see saris and sombreros, yarmulkes and backward ball caps. I can see gorgeous neck coils and colorful turbans. I can see conical hats and kimonos and Converse. I can smell poi from Hawaii, pirozhki from Russia, arepas from Venezuela, gyros from Greece, congee from Taiwan and curries from Jamaica and India. I can hear English, Spanish, Swahili, Japanese, Italian, French, Hebrew, Turkish and Mandarin. I hear Native American drums, and I see Hawaiian and Polynesian dancers. That's a glimpse of the kingdom of God![2]

When we travel down the road toward reconciliation, *this* is what awaits us: the colorful tapestry of humanity in all of its rich, God-breathed variety. This innumerable crowd of crosscultural witnesses foretold in Revelation will bring the glory and honor of their nations into the city of God (Revelation 21:24). Their convergence will be like the streams of a great, life-giving river that will flow through the middle of the city of God. Trees will grow on each side of this river, and "the leaves of the tree are for the healing of the nations" (Revelation 22:2). This is the vision that Dr. Martin Luther King Jr. referred to as the "Beloved Community"—a completely integrated society, a community of love and justice wherein equality, unity and justice will be an actuality, not just a dream.

LIVING THE VISION

Several years ago I started a coaching network for pastors of multicultural churches called the VIBE Alliance, which stands for Victory in Breaking Ethnocentrism. These pastors came from different cities in the United States with a common calling to build diverse churches that are committed to reconciliation. They met with me for a year to learn practices and principles of effective multiethnic ministry based on the Reconciliation Roadmap. Three of the pastors in the network have gone on to lead churches that are doing a remarkable job of living out this model in their local contexts. They are Peter Ahn, Daniel Hill and David Swanson, whose stories I featured earlier in this book. So let's review some of the specific ways these leaders have put the Reconciliation Roadmap into practice.

First, they have successfully navigated their churches through *catalytic events*, such as losing key ethnic minority leaders, that could have severely divided the church. They have also examined their organizational culture to determine what structures and policies helped or hindered their desire for reconciliation. This *realization* enabled them to address unconscious power dynamics in the church so that people from different cultures could encounter each other with equal strength. In addition, they made sure that their value for reconciliation and multiethnic ministry is clearly articulated in their vision and mission statements. To join these churches is to know exactly what they stand for!

As their churches have continued to grow, the pastors have encouraged *identification* throughout the congregation by varying their worship styles, celebrating different ethnic cultures and empowering men and women equally to serve in leadership. They also have built authentic relationships with their neighbors and are connected to the needs of their local communities. These three senior pastors are all committed to the biblical value of reconciliation and preach and teach on it regularly. Also, as a part of the *preparation* process, they mentor and train their leaders to minister from a place of intercultural awareness and sensitivity.

When it comes to the *activation phase*, each of these churches is committed to its local community and is an advocate and ally for justice and social change. They publicly stand up and speak out on issues of unity and reconciliation. They are active in their communities, building trust and demonstrating their credibility by partnering with organizations and local leaders to address systemic issues over an extended period. They are advocates and allies, not just churches taking up space in their communities. They each have a positive relationship with the public schools and the principals in their neighborhood to improve the education system for all children.

These three churches, made up of people from different racial, ethnic, cultural and socioeconomic backgrounds, are "practicing what they preach"! Don't get me wrong: they're not perfect, but they are impressive. They are shining examples for me of what the Reconciliation Roadmap can look like.

THE POWER TO BRING SHALOM

Once you begin, you should never again resemble the people you once were. You will always bear the marks of your transformation. The Reconciliation Roadmap gives you some guidance and a few landmarks as you seek to partner with God in the ongoing work of mending the brokenness of humanity. Following the Roadmap will enable you to build entirely new reconciled communities; communities of shalom; communities where nothing is broken and no one is missing.

I know that this kind of change takes time and that the Beloved Community is "both now and not yet." It's here in part, ushered in by Jesus, but it isn't yet here in full. This vision won't be fully realized until Jesus Christ returns, but in the meantime, we have been invited by God to create reconciled communities that become microcosms of the kingdom on earth. Our ongoing collective participation in the process of reconciliation can transform our society into a place where shalom becomes a greater reality and all people can thrive.

Our Beloved Community might still be a long way off. But like Dr. King, I believe that it will eventually be actualized and that we can already see glimpses of it here and now. We can be the bell ringers. We can point the way and show others what it looks like. My hope isn't that we change the social order but instead that, like Jesus and his disciples, we build small cadres of the Beloved Community that can infiltrate society and change it from the inside out over time. Our collective calling is to make the kingdom of God visible on earth. Every time we bridge racial, ethnic, gender and socioeconomic divides, we become prophetic witnesses to the reality of the kingdom of God. In small and big ways we give people glimpses of what the future vision looks like. This is our mission, and we must never lose hope, knowing that God has the power to bring the kingdom—on earth as it is in heaven. God has the power to bring shalom.

STAY ON THE JOURNEY

We all want to give our lives for something that really matters. As human beings, we want to know that our lives have meaning and purpose. By giving ourselves to the great vision of what God is doing in the world, we find our significance in this bigger story. It's God's desire that each of us be a part of healing humanity. When we take the courageous journey to discover our true selves, reconcile with others and live into God's purpose, we become agents of change and transformation in a world that desperately needs healing. The journey transforms us into change agents who positively influence the society around us.

People are changed more by experience than by information. I've always thought that to be true, but I believed it even more when I went on a journey with a group of women leaders from the Evangelical Covenant Church to retrace the civil rights movement. One of our first stops was in Birmingham, Alabama, where we visited the church and sat in the Sunday school classroom where four little girls were killed by a bomb planted by a white supremacist. We also visited a civil rights museum that had an interactive exhibit titled "I Was There," where people could leave brief notes saying how they participated in or supported the fight for racial equality. After that we went to Selma, Alabama, where we walked across the Edmund Pettus Bridge and reenacted what it must have been like to march toward certain doom with each step forward on Bloody Sunday.

Our next stop was in Smithville, Georgia, where we met an

African American woman named Sandra, who was close to my age. When she was eleven, she marched with Martin Luther King, was arrested and remained in jail for three weeks—and *nobody notified her mother!* Sandra told us that when she woke up the morning of the march, she said, "Momma, today I'm willing to die for my people." After she was arrested, one of the jailers treated her with kindness and gave her a sandwich every day, but for three weeks her mother had no idea where she was. Can you imagine? At eleven years old she wanted to be a part of securing her own rights and the rights of others, and she was willing to face the consequences—even death—to do so. As I listened to her, I began to wonder—*what was I doing when she was fighting for her rights (our rights) in 1968?* That year I was thirteen. If she was being arrested at eleven, what was I doing at thirteen? I felt like I had missed a whole part of history in which I should have participated. Maybe it was because I was born in the North and not the South; nevertheless, I had not taken part in something that should have been important to me.

From Smithville our journey took us to Atlanta, Georgia, where we found ourselves at the King Center the very week that Coretta Scott King died. In fact, we had the opportunity to attend one of the memorial services that was being held at Ebenezer Baptist Church, where Dr. King was once pastor. At first I was daunted by the size of the crowd trying to get into this small church for the service. I almost decided not to go, because it seemed useless to try to contend with all of the people trying to get inside. While I was contemplating what to do, my husband called to ask how the trip was going. As we talked about my experiences, I was so filled with awe at the opportunity to participate in *this* part of history that with tears streaming down my face, I told my husband: "For most of my life, history was made and I did not participate, but this time, if somebody asks me where I was when Coretta Scott King died, I want to say, 'I was there!'"

You never know when all of the facts that you have learned in life may coalesce to become an experience. It might seem small to you, but attending the memorial service for Coretta Scott King was one of the high moments of my life. Walking hand in hand across the Edmund Pettus Bridge was eerie and powerful, and I'll never forget the hollow in my stomach as I walked through the Sixteenth Street Baptist Church, but my real epiphany came when I met Sandra. Listening to her, I became more aware of the fact that history was being made all along, and women and children were a significant part of making history, like she did when she walked with Dr. King. I know now that I never want to miss any part of history again.

Rev. Martin Luther King Jr. is widely quoted as saying, "Most people are thermometers that record or register the temperature of majority opinion, not thermostats that transform and regulate the temperature of society." The Reconciliation Roadmap allows us the chance to be thermostats instead of thermometers. It brings us into contact with the essence of what God is doing in the world and allows us to be active in the transformation of society. So I challenge you to keep pressing in and to stay always on the journey. I challenge you to seek shalom with the whole of your life, and as you do, I pray that this Franciscan benediction will be true of you and your community as you go.

May God bless you with discomfort at easy answers, half-truths, and superficial relationships so that you may live deep within your heart.

May God bless you with anger at injustice, oppression, and exploitation of people, so that you may work for justice, freedom and peace.

May God bless you with tears to shed for those who suffer pain, rejection, hunger and war, so that you may reach out your hand to comfort them and to turn their pain into joy.

And may God bless you with enough foolishness to believe that you can make a difference in the world, so that you can do what others claim cannot be done to bring justice and kindness to all our children and the poor.

Amen.[3]

ACKNOWLEDGMENTS

There is no one, besides God, that I thank more for this book than my husband, J. Derek McNeil. For years we worked on this project together, and his wisdom and intellectual insights into human behavior and systemic change are reflected throughout the pages of this book.

In addition, special thanks goes to Nancy Myers Rust, my writing assistant, and Ashley June Moore, my study partner, who faithfully labored with me for hours in libraries and coffee shops to write this book. I will never cease to thank God for your support, dedication, commitment to excellence and attention to detail as we pressed toward the finish line. You were the "midwives" who helped to make this book a reality, and there are no words to adequately express how much I love and appreciate you for all your creativity and hard work.

Cindy Bunch, my editor at InterVarsity Press, also deserves a world of praise. Her confidence in me as an author gave me the freedom to find my voice, to speak my truth and to say what I most honestly wanted to say. Every suggestion she made that challenged me to dig deeper and give more was right and greatly improved the overall quality and usefulness of this book. I could not be more grateful for her partnership in ministry. Thanks also to my wonderful publishing family at IVP including Deborah Gonzalez, Jeff Crosby and Bob Fryling.

Along the way there have been others who have also believed with me for the completion of this book. No one fits this description more than Rosanne Swain! She prayed and encouraged me to write this book, even in the midst of major life challenges and transitions. She never lost sight of the vision and knew the significance and importance of writing for the work God has called me to. I am absolutely sure that this finished product is her harvest.

Similarly, I am indebted to Doug Slaybaugh, who helped me to clarify my mission statement and challenged me to write what he called a "manifesto" that summarized my work. This one is for you, Doug! Thank you. I am also deeply grateful for the input I received from my children, Omari and Mia McNeil, whose invaluable insight helped me to better understand this generation of young, emerging leaders.

Special thanks to my executive assistant, Carol Quinlan, who adds immense value to my life and ministry. Thank you for protecting my time and handling a multitude of details to make it possible for me to write this book. I am also deeply grateful for Betzy Cisneros and Susie Becker, who worked with me for years to refine the ideas in this book as we served churches, colleges and organizations through Salter McNeil & Associates.

I am especially thankful for my friends, who understand that this book represents my life's work. To Ruth Haley Barton, who has walked with me every step of the way, I thank you for the gift of your love and companionship on this journey. To my pastor, Eugene Cho, thank you for your wise counsel and strategic guidance along the way. Also my deepest thanks go to Daniel Hill, David Swanson and Nate Grossman for reading this manuscript and giving me valuable feedback and insights that have helped to raise the caliber of this book to a higher level. You have enriched my life as I have had the privilege of walking alongside you in ministry. To my sister-girl, Gail Song Bantum, thank you for always having my back and for providing me with such powerful quotes for this book. Finally, I am deeply grateful to my Intercessory Prayer Team, who faithfully support me in prayer; and to Rick Richardson, who prayed over me many years ago and said that "much would be published through this ministry." Thank you for your prophetic words that still inspire me and continue to bear fruit in my life today.

In closing, I had no idea how much I would enjoy being a college professor! Thank you to all my students at Seattle Pacific University for making our classroom a laboratory where we learn, clarify and apply these ideas together. I am particularly grateful to Brian Gregory and my seminary students in THEO 6513, who helped me to choose the title for this book. I promised that I'd mention you and I do so with great joy!

For all this and more I give all the glory to God!

NOTES

CHAPTER ONE: WHAT IS RECONCILIATION?

[1]This conversation took place at the 2010 National Multiethnic Church Conference.

[2]Anthony C. Thiselton, *Interpreting God and the Postmodern Self* (Grand Rapids: Eerdmans, 1995). Thiselton suggests that the "pouring out" of the Holy Spirit on all people (Acts 2:17) is a reversal of Babel, and it fulfills the promise in Joel 2:28-29.

[3]The story is told in Mary-Anne Plaatjies Van Huffel, "The Belhar Confession: Born in the Struggle Against Apartheid in Southern Africa," http://uir.unisa.ac.za/bitstream/handle/10500/9977/Plaatjies_Van_Huffel _11.pdf?sequence=1.

CHAPTER TWO: LANDMARKS OF RECONCILIATION

[1]Marilynn B. Brewer and Norman Miller, *Intergroup Relations* (Pacific Grove, CA: Brooks/Cole, 1996), 7.

CHAPTER THREE: SHAKE IT UP!

[1]John Paul Lederach, *The Moral Imagination: The Art and Soul of Building Peace* (New York: Oxford University Press, 2005), 21-29.

[2]Bruce E. Wexler, *Brain and Culture: Neurobiology, Ideology, and Social Change* (Cambridge, MA: MIT Press, 2006).

[3]Ibid., 196.

[4]Ibid., 7.

[5]Edgar Schein, quoted in Diane Coutu, "The Anxiety of Learning," *Harvard Business Review*, March 2002, http://hbr.org/2002/03/the-anxiety-of -learning.

[6]Ibid.

[7]M. Scott Peck, *The Different Drum: Community Making and Peace* (New York: Touchstone, 1987), 86-103.

CHAPTER FOUR: A SHIFT IN PERSPECTIVE

[1]Anne Lamott, *Help, Thanks, Wow* (New York: Riverhead Books, 2012), 86.

CHAPTER FIVE: A GROUP EFFORT

[1]Andy Dunn, "Creating a Strong Company Culture," *Business of Fashion*, April 29, 2014, www.businessoffashion.com/2014/04/creating-culture -andy-dunn-bonobos.html.

[2]John P. Kotter, *Leading Change* (Boston: Harvard Business School Press, 1996).

[3]Ruth Haley Barton, *Life Together in Christ: Experiencing Transformation in Community* (Downers Grove, IL: InterVarsity Press, 2014), 38.

[4]John M. Gottman and Joan DeClaire, *The Relationship Cure: A 5 Step Guide to Strengthening Your Marriage, Family, and Friendships* (New York: Three Rivers, 2001).

CHAPTER SIX: PLANNING FOR ACTION

[1]Brian McLaren, "Q & R: You, Rob Bell, Don Miller, and Christianity Today," 2014, http://brianmclaren.net/q-r-you-rob-bell-don-miller-and -christianity-today/.

[2]C. Otto Scharmer, *Theory U: Leading from the Future as It Emerges* (San Francisco: Berrett-Koehler, 2009), summary of chap. 11.

[3]Margaret J. Wheatley, *Leadership and the New Science: Discovering Order in a Chaotic World* (San Francisco: Berrett-Koehler, 1999), 146.

[4]"Leadership and Institutional Change," National Academy for Academic Leadership, n.d., http://www.thenationalacademy.org/ready/change.html.

CHAPTER SEVEN: DOING JUSTICE

[1]Eric H. F. Law, *The Wolf Shall Dwell with the Lamb: A Spirituality for Leadership in a Multicultural Community* (St. Louis: Chalice, 1993), 13.

[2]Ibid., 14.

[3]Ibid., 27.

[4]Vernon Johns, in Patrick Louis Cooney's summary of the film *The Road to Freedom: The Vernon Johns Story* (dir. Kenneth Fink), n.d., www .vernonjohns.org/snuffy1186/vernjohn.html.

CHAPTER EIGHT: REPAIRING BROKEN SYSTEMS TOGETHER

[1]Jennifer Harvey, *Dear White Christians: For Those Still Longing for Racial Reconciliation* (Grand Rapids: Eerdmans, 2014), 170.

CHAPTER NINE: STAYING THE COURSE

[1]For more information about PathLight, please visit its website: http://pathlight.org.

[2]"The Five-fold Test," The Evangelical Covenant Church, n.d., www.covenant companion.com/wp-content/uploads/2018/07/Five-fold-Test.pdf.

CONCLUSION: A VISION OF A FLOURISHING FUTURE

[1]Eric H. F. Law, *The Wolf Shall Dwell with the Lamb: A Spirituality for Leadership in a Multicultural Community* (St. Louis: Chalice, 1993), 14.

[2]Adapted from a blog post by Nancy Myers Rust, www.therustylife.com.

[3]Adapted from "A Franciscan Benediction," The Epistle, n.d., http://epistle .us/inspiration/franciscanbenediction.html.

ALSO BY BRENDA SALTER McNEIL

A Credible Witness: Reflections on Power,
Evangelism and Race

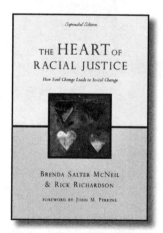

The Heart of Racial Justice: How Soul
Change Leads to Social Change
coauthored by Rick Richardson

A CALL TO ACTION

From Dr. Brenda Salter McNeil

For many of us, discovering the next step is often an intimidating task. But I am here to tell you that **you don't have to do it alone!**

As part of the Roadmap to Reconciliation program, I have created a process to help you begin the journey to take action.

Visit **www.saltermcneil.com** to discover how to bring these reconciliation strategies and practices to your local church, organization, or ministry context.

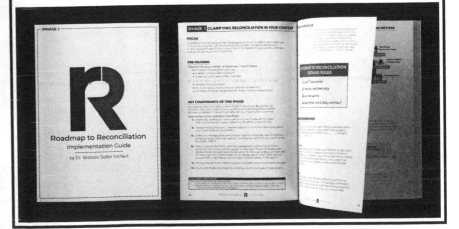

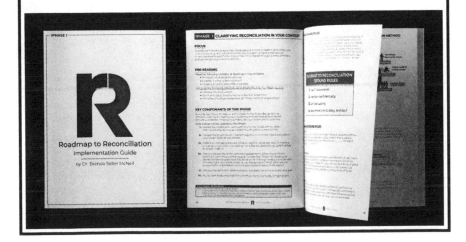